The Blueprint

Building Powerful Special Education Practices

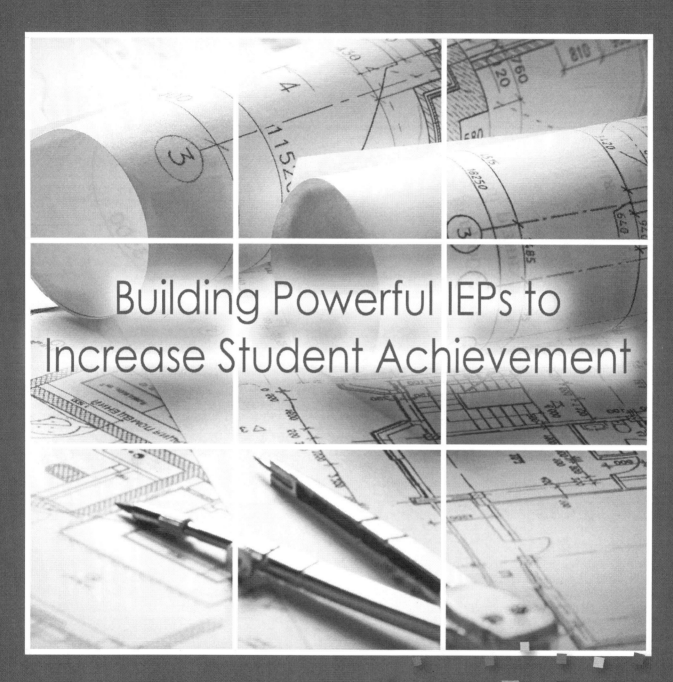

Building Powerful IEPs to Increase Student Achievement

CREC | Expert Solutions

Winners make a habit of manufacturing their own positive expectations in advance of the event.

~ Brian Tracy

TABLE OF CONTENTS

About the Authors 4

Introduction 5

Module 1: *Determining Present Levels of Academic Achievement and Functional Performance (PLAAFP)* 13

What do you know about PLAAFP? – Answer Key 17
Key Ideas 18
Present Level of Academic and Functional Performance (PLAAFP) Guidance 19
PLAAFP Study Guide – Answer Key 22
Parent and Student Input 24
Special Education 32
Creating the Impact Statement 33
Educational Benefit Protocol .39

Module 2: *Writing Standards-Based Individual Education Plans (IEPs)* 45

Characteristics of a Standards-Based IEP 49
Measurable Annual Goals 55
Goals 56
Objectives 59
Special Education 62
Measuring and Reporting Progress 64

Module 3: *Creating Instruction from the Common Core Standards for Special Education and Related Services* 67

Common Core Standards (CCS) 69
Instructional Shifts – ELA 75
Specially Designed Instruction 84
Universal Design for Learning 90
Modifications and Accommodations 99
Specially Designed Instruction 105

Module 4: *Collecting Data and Monitoring of the IEP Progress* 113

Progress Monitoring: Assessment, Data Collection and Informing Instruction and Practice 115
SMART Goals and Objectives 135
The PLAAFP and IEP Goals 138
Resources for Finding the Most Up-To-Date Data
  Collection Tools 151

Online Resources 162

Bibliography 163

Glossary 167

ABOUT THE AUTHORS

The Blueprint: Building Powerful IEPs to Increase Student Achievement modules were developed and field tested by a talented group of Education Specialists in CREC's Technical Assistance and Brokering Services (TABS) Division. It is through their dedication and expertise we are able to provide a comprehensive training curriculum that will assist educators in developing and implementing powerful IEPs. The following CREC educational specialists not only developed the curriculum, but have trained hundreds of educators in the IEP Blueprint.

Lisa A. Fiano, Technical Assistance & Brokering Services (TABS), CREC
Julie Giaccone, Technical Assistance & Brokering Services (TABS), CREC
Sonya Kunkel, Technical Assistance & Brokering Services (TABS), CREC

Project Staff:

Denise Gable, Technical Assistance & Brokering Services (TABS), CREC
Cindy Lang, Technical Assistance & Brokering Services (TABS), CREC
Tricia Silva, Technical Assistance & Brokering Services (TABS), CREC
Tom Sullivan, Tecnical Assistance & Brokering Services (TABS), CREC

Contributors:

Many people contributed to the creation of **The Blueprint** Modules. These individuals are doing remarkable work with students and schools. We thank each of them for contributing their expertise to this body of work for special education teachers and related service personnel.

Elizabeth Battaglia, Ed. D
Kerri Brown, Ph.D.
Alison Cianciolo
Tonja Kelly
Margaret MacDonald, Ph.D.

Donna Morelli
Nicole Natale
Mary Jo Terranova
Cynthia Zingler

INTRODUCTION

The Blueprint modules are designed to assist IEP teams in creating an IEP that is "reasonably calculated to result in educational benefit" (Rhinebeck, 1996) for students who receive special education services. This series of modules explicitly instructs IEP teams how to create the components of the IEP so that the individual pieces link together in a scope and sequence fashion to form an appropriate educational program for students with disabilities. Just like a house requires a well thought out blueprint, a good education program requires a well thought out IEP. **The Blueprint** training curriculum has been written to allow trainers to customize according to state and district requirements. You should adjust or substitute information to comply with local legal requirements. Verify all legal information with your local counsel, board, administration, compliance officers and school attorneys.

The curriculum of **The Blueprint** is research based in both design and instructional outcomes. Elements of the design include:

- Evidence based curriculum design model from the University of Kansas Center for Research on Learning Strategic Instruction Model

- Review by recognized experts in the field of standards-based IEP development and educational benefit

- Field testing in public schools

Module Description

Design of an effective IEP is similar to designing a building. The building will only be as good as its blueprint and a students' educational program will only be as good as their IEP. We chose to call this training curriculum **The Blueprint** to represent the importance that proper IEP design has on instruction and student achievement.

The modules will move the learner from development of present levels of performance all the way through the monitoring of student progress. There are four modules, each providing three to six hours of training. We recommend that they be provided in module order.

This is an overview of the four Blueprint modules. This organizer is an example of the research-based Unit Organizer strategy from the University of Kansas. This advanced organizer prepares you for the content that will be covered in these modules.

The Unit Organizer

The Blueprint: Building Powerful IEPs to Increase Student Achievement

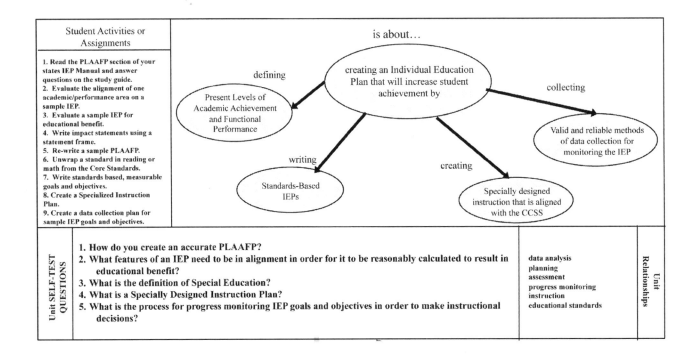

Student Activities or Assignments
1. Read the PLAAFP section of your states IEP Manual and answer questions on the study guide. 2. Evaluate the alignment of one academic/performance area on a sample IEP. 3. Evaluate a sample IEP for educational benefit. 4. Write impact statements using a statement frame. 5. Re-write a sample PLAAFP. 6. Unwrap a standard in reading or math from the Core Standards. 7. Write standards based, measurable goals and objectives. 8. Create a Specialized Instruction Plan. 9. Create a data collection plan for sample IEP goals and objectives.

is about...

defining

creating an Individual Education Plan that will increase student achievement by

collecting

Present Levels of Academic Achievement and Functional Performance

Valid and reliable methods of data collection for monitoring the IEP

writing

creating

Standards-Based IEPs

Specially designed instruction that is aligned with the CCSS

Unit SELF-TEST QUESTIONS

1. How do you create an accurate PLAAFP?
2. What features of an IEP need to be in alignment in order for it to be reasonably calculated to result in educational benefit?
3. What is the definition of Special Education?
4. What is a Specially Designed Instruction Plan?
5. What is the process for progress monitoring IEP goals and objectives in order to make instructional decisions?

data analysis
planning
assessment
progress monitoring
instruction
educational standards

Unit Relationships

Module 1 Defining Present Levels of Academic Achievement and Functional Performance (PLAAFP)

This module discusses the PLAAFP that is the heart of the IEP. Module 1 reviews the process of analyzing student data to establish a baseline of academic achievement and/or functional performance, identifying strengths and concerns and accurately describing the impact of the student's disability on their performance in the general education curriculum. Opportunities to review sample PLAAFP forms and to practice writing impact statements are part of this module.

The lesson organizer provides an overview of the challenge questions, tasks and learning outcomes for **The Blueprint** Module 1, *Defining Present Levels of Academic Achievement and Functional Performance (PLAAFP).*

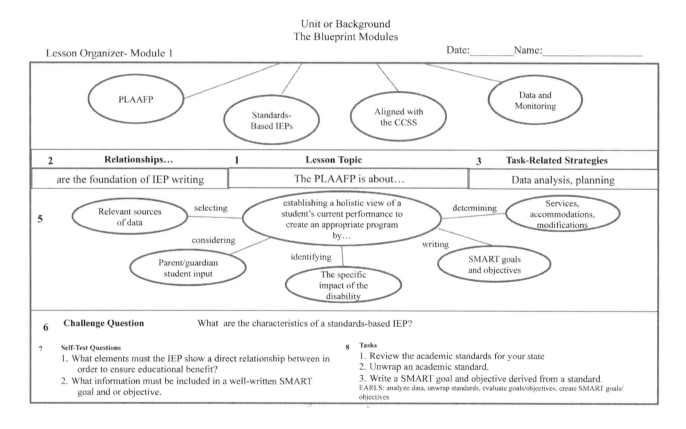

Module 2 Writing Standards-Based IEPs

In Module 2, educators learn to identify suitable grade level expectations based on student performance in order to write goals and objectives. Educators will practice unwrapping standards and writing goals and objectives that are observable and measurable. The end result is to create a document that will lead to instructional planning by embedding the necessary specially designed instruction into instruction in the general education classroom.

The lesson organizer provides the challenge questions, tasks and learning outcomes for **The Blueprint** Module 2, *Writing Standards-Based IEPs.*

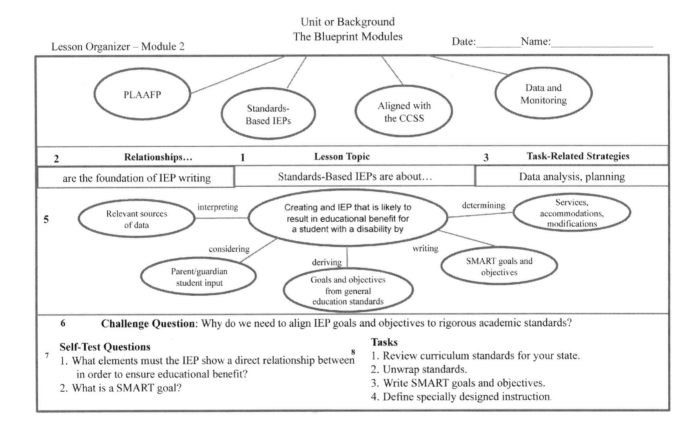

Module 3 Creating Instruction from the Common Core Standards for Special Education and Related Services

The third module takes standards-based goals and objectives and turns them into instructional plans in light of the instructional implications of the high expectations of current educational standards. Educational personnel will learn to use Universal Design for Learning, accommodations, planning matrices and lesson templates to create instructional plans that can be used by both general and special educators on behalf of students with disabilities.

The lesson organizer provides the challenge questions, tasks and learning outcomes for **The Blueprint** Module 3, *Creating Instruction from the Common Core Standards for Special Education and Related Services.*

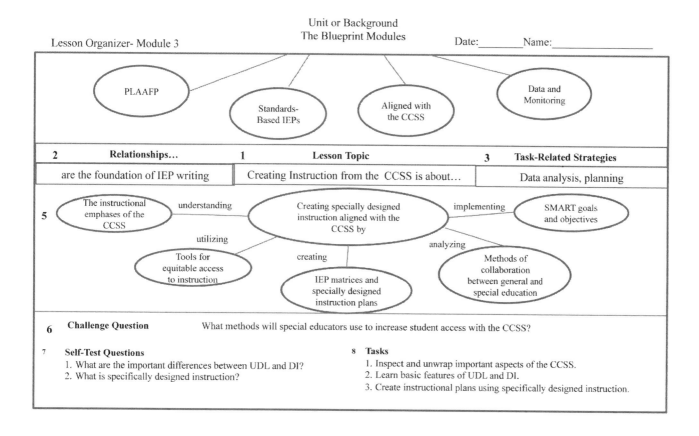

Module 4 Data Collection and Monitoring of the IEP Progress

The last module outlines methods of IEP progress monitoring to ensure that the individual student makes growth. A variety of progress monitoring and data collection tools will be explored in this module. Teachers and related service personnel will learn how to establish a data collection schedule, select appropriate data collection tools, and analyze data trends to make instructional decisions.

The lesson organizer provides the challenge questions, tasks and learning outcomes for **The Blueprint** Module 4, *Data Collection and Monitoring of the IEP Progress.*

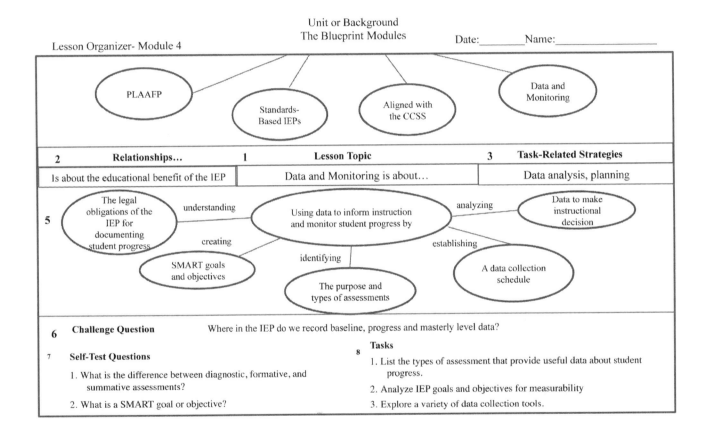

Using the The Blueprint Workbook

This workbook is meant to help educators learn and practice the skills that are introduced in the four modules of **The Blueprint: Building Powerful IEPs to Increase Student Achievement**. You will be asked to use some strategies to reflect on your success.

Who can use the Workbook?

This workbook is designed for anyone who is a practicing or aspiring educator.

Benefits of the Workbook

The workbook activities are aligned with **The Blueprint** training curriculum. As you complete the workbook, you will be demonstrating competencies and the workbook serves as a portfolio of your learning and growth. If you are an aspiring educator, childcare worker or teacher, the workbook will show potential employees your strengths and will prepare you for your new job. As an experienced educator, you can use the workbook to demonstrate growth to your employer and help you to remember and refer to important key concepts.

How The Blueprint Workbook is organized

This workbook is designed to accompany the four **Blueprint** Modules. While it can be used alone, you will benefit most from participating in **The Blueprint** training and using the workbook as a companion. The workbook is organized as a partner for **The Blueprint** training and is aligned with **The Blueprint** Modules. We recommend that you work through the modules in order, as in some cases information builds from one module to the next.

Completion of Activities in The Blueprint Workbook

You are invited on numerous occasions to try a variety of activities and then to reflect on their success. Try to answer the questions posed honestly and follow through on your action plans. Sharing your workbook with others will assist you in your own learning and growth. You will be given information that will assist you as an educator. At the end of each module there is a quiz and a reflection paper to assist you in your learning.

Building Powerful IEPs to Increase Student Achievement

Module 1:

Determining Present Levels of Academic Achievement and Functional Performance (PLAAFP)

In this Module you will

- ✓ Identify and prioritize appropriate sources of assessment data.

- ✓ Use data to establish current baselines and performance levels.

- ✓ Define adverse effect of disability on current educational performance.

- ✓ Use guidelines to write useful statement of impact of disability to determine appropriate goals and objectives.

- ✓ Effectively use parent/guardian and student input.

Module 1 Defining Present Levels of Academic Achievement and Functional Performance (PLAAFP)

The illiterate of the 21st century will not be those who cannot read and write, but those who cannot learn, unlearn, and relearn.

– ALVIN TOFFLER

This quote was selected because educators have been asked to change the way they write IEPs. As a profession, we need to be adaptable and respond to new ways to meet student needs. For example, we need to write our IEP documents in alignment with a Response to Intervention (RtI) framework, and to the Common Core Standards. Students must receive "educational benefit" from the specialized services dictated by the IEP.

Unit or Background
The Blueprint Modules

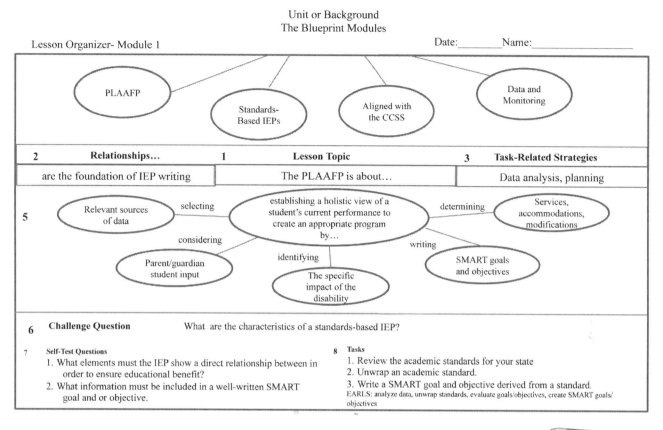

Lesson Organizer- Module 1   Date:_____ Name:_____

2	Relationships...	1	Lesson Topic	3	Task-Related Strategies
are the foundation of IEP writing		The PLAAFP is about...		Data analysis, planning	

5

Relevant sources of data — *selecting* — establishing a holistic view of a student's current performance to create an appropriate program by... — *determining* — Services, accommodations, modifications

considering — Parent/guardian student input

identifying — The specific impact of the disability

writing — SMART goals and objectives

6   Challenge Question   What are the characteristics of a standards-based IEP?

7   Self-Test Questions
   1. What elements must the IEP show a direct relationship between in order to ensure educational benefit?
   2. What information must be included in a well-written SMART goal and or objective.

8   Tasks
   1. Review the academic standards for your state.
   2. Unwrap an academic standard.
   3. Write a SMART goal and objective derived from a standard.
   EARLS: analyze data, unwrap standards, evaluate goals/objectives, create SMART goals/objectives

Questions I Hope Get Answered

What are the questions or concerns you have about the PLAAFP that you hope will be addressed?

Activity: What Do You Know About PLAAFP?

Directions: Take 3-4 minutes to mark the statements on the Anticipation Guide as True or False, then go to the next page and compare your answers to the correct answers.

The PLAAFP only describes what a child with a disability knows and is able to do.   **T F**

Present levels of performance should come from standardized test data.   **T F**

All areas of the PLAAFP must be aligned including goals and objectives.   **T F**

A concern or need leads to goals and objectives when it requires specially designed instruction.   **T F**

Parent input is required on the PLAAFP.   **T F**

Student strengths should be included in each performance area.   **T F**

What do you know about PLAAFP? – Answer Key

(Answers in *BOLD ITALIC*)

Directions: Read each of the statements before beginning the PLAAFP workshop. Circle True (T) or False (F) for each of the statements. You can correct or confirm each of your answers as you go through the workshop or at the end of the session.

1. The PLAAFP describes what a child with a disability knows and is able to do.
   True

2. Present levels of performance should only come from standardized test data.
   False

3. All areas of the PLAAFP must be aligned including goals and objectives.
   True

4. A concern or need leads to goals and objectives when it requires specially designed instruction.
   True

5. Parent input is required on the PLAAFP.
   True

6. Student strengths should be included in each performance area.
   True

Reflection

- What did you learn that you didn't know?

Education Benefit

An IEP must show a direct relationship between:

- present levels of academic achievement and functional performance
- impact of the disability on progress and participation in the curriculum
- goals
- the type and amount of services provided
- accommodations and modifications needed
- assessment of progress toward mastery of goals (and objectives, if applicable)

The diagram above describes how an IEP must be constructed in order for it to be reasonably calculated to result in educational benefit for a child.

Key Ideas

- Selecting relevant sources of data to determine a student's present level of performance.

- Parental input.

- Identifying the impact of the student's disability to develop appropriate goals and objectives.

The Blueprint: Building Powerful IEPs to Increase Student Achievement

Determining Education Benefit

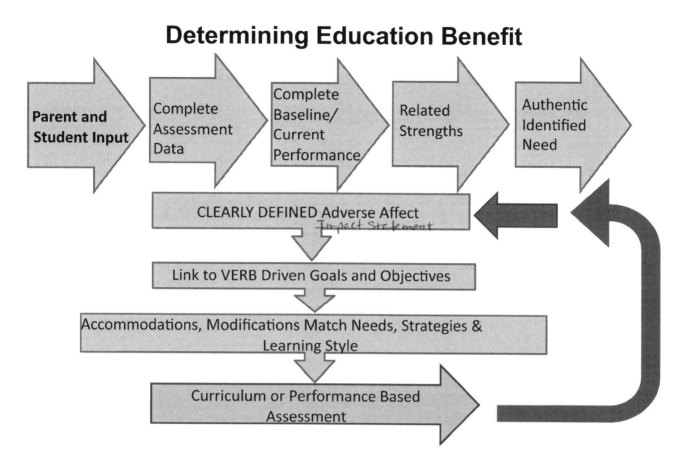

The Determining Educational Benefit graphic is a visual representation of how educational benefit is created. Elements are depicted that will result in a PLAAFP to ensure an IEP that is reasonably calculated to result in educational benefit.

Present Level of Academic and Functional Performance (PLAAFP) Guidance

Reflection

- What source(s) do you currently use to guide your PLAAFP description?

- How do you know what to write?

Activity

The purpose of this activity is for you to become familiar with the way a state has defined PLAAFP.

Directions:

- ✓ Please go to your state resource for IEP development and answer the questions on the Study Guide below. If you are from Connecticut or cannot find your state's information, The Connecticut Manual and Present Level of Academic Achievement and Functional Performance Form can be found at the website below. http://www.sde.ct.gov/sde/lib/sde/PDF/DEPS/Special/IEPManual.pdf

- ✓ Read pages that refer to the PLAAFP.

- ✓ Use the Study Guide to answer the questions about the important aspects of the PLAAFP form.

- ✓ When you are done, compare your answers to the Study Guide Answer Key.

PLAAFP Study Guide

1. PLAAFP stands for ...

2. List nine ways by which you can view the student's current performance.

3. The PLAAFP helps define the need for ...

4. Parent input should always be included in the development of the PLAAFP.
   T or F

5. Define the following sections of the PLAAFP:

   a. Academic and Functional Performance Areas

   b. Strengths

   c. Concerns/Needs

   d. Impact

PLAAFP Study Guide – Answer Key

Answers in *ITALICS*

1. PLAAFP stands for…

   Present Levels of Academic Achievement and Functional Performance

2. List the means by which you can view the student's current performance holistically.

   a. *curriculum based measurements*

   b. *running records*

   c. *portfolios*

   d. *student work*

   e. *standardized assessments*

   f. *district and state assessments*

   g. *classroom observations*

   h. *parent and student input*

   i. *teacher input*

3. The PLAAFP helps define the need for ...

   The PLAAPP defines the need for specially designed instruction and determines how that specially designed instruction should look in terms of goals, supports, and services.

4. Parent input should always be included in the development of the PLAAFP. True or False

   (Answer = True)

5. Define the following sections of the PLAAFP.

a. Academic and Functional Performance Areas-

The statements written in this area should clearly articulate what the student currently knows and can do in relationship to his/her involvement and progress in general curriculum or appropriate preschool/early childhood activities.

b. Strengths – Participants may select any one of the sentences below.

Strengths may include a relatively strong area for the student; a strength when compared to peers, or particular motivational or interest area. Statements about the student's strengths can support instructional decisions related to motivation, learning styles, and learning preferences. If the student's strength is supported by the used of supplemental aids and services including assistive technology, the PPT can record that information.

c. Concerns/Needs-

The concerns/needs detailed in this area which have a marked impact on the child's educational performance and requires specially designed instruction should result in a corresponding annual goal.

d. Impact-

Describe how the student's disability specifically impacts her/his involvement and progress in the general curriculum or participation in appropriate preschool/early childhood activities.

Parent and Student Input

Input from parent and student should be specifically recorded on the PLAAFP.

Example: Julie has difficulty reading homework and other books by herself. She cannot sound out the words and also seems to hold the book very closely to her eyes.

Reflection

- What are some other examples of appropriate parent/student input that could be recorded here?

- What positive statements should be included?

- Why is this important?

- What is the intent of this section?

Tips for Non-Communicative Parents:

1. Take your value system out of the exchange.

2. Maintain relaxed body language.

3. Stay focused on the needs of the child.

4. Always start with positive comments.

5. Note growth.

Academic and Functional Performance Areas

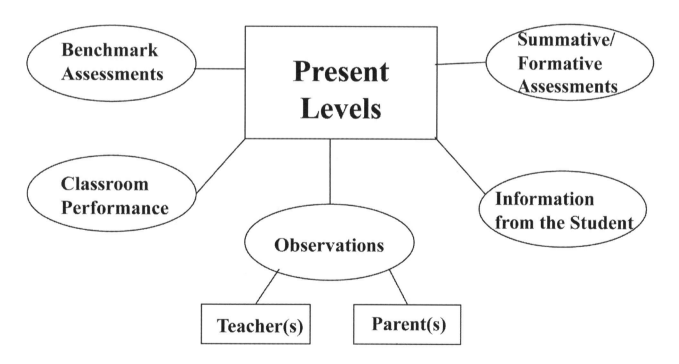

Activity

Directions: Review the *Academic and Functional Performance Areas* graphic and generate a list of data sources that an educator can use when creating a student PLAAFP.

✓

✓

✓

Here are some sources of data for the PLAAFP from www.Texasprojectfirst.org:

- Work Samples

- Photographs

- Video Tape

- Behavioral Data

- Parent Communication

- Standardized Assessment

    ✓ A standardized assessment (or test) is a test administered and scored in a consistent manner. The tests are designed in such a way that the "questions, conditions for administering, scoring procedures, and interpretations are consistent" and are "administered and scored in a predetermined, standard manner." These types of assessments are typically used in schools to compare a student to his/her peers

- Anecdotal Records

    ✓ An informal, written record (usually positive in tone), based on the observations of the teacher, of a student's progress and/or activities which occur throughout the day.

- Narrative Records

- ✓ Records that are written in a "story" form intended to provide a more or less faithful reproduction of behavior or observations as it originally occurred.

- Statewide Assessments

- Benchmark Assessments

  - ✓ A standard by which something is evaluated or measured. Typically "benchmarks" may be established several times during a school year and used to determine progress or the lack of progress in a given skill.

- Teacher-made tests

- Attendance Data

- District Wide Tests

- Portfolios

Complete Assessment Data

- What data is available and relevant in determining present levels of student performance?

- How do we "mine" the data?

Reflection

- Given all of the data that is available, how do we determine what the data is telling us about the student?

- How do we determine what data is most relevant in establishing the student's current levels of performance, strengths and concerns in a particular performance area?

- Why is it important for teachers and related service personnel to understand that analyzing the data is much more important than simply listing a series of scores?

- What data sources should be used to determine eligibility, continued eligibility, areas of need and areas of strength?

- What are your state's regulations?

- What sources of data does your district currently use?

- How might those sources of data change as determination of eligibility shifts to a Response to Intervention model?

The Blueprint: Building Powerful IEPs to Increase Student Achievement
All Rights Reserved/ www.crec.org

Activity

Generate a list of data sources used in your district.

EXAMPLE: A student has a DRA Level of 40 (Developmental Reading Assessment). What does this score tell me about what the student knows and can do? How does it help me to determine the authentic identified need in the area of reading that rises to the level of requiring specially designed instruction?

Reflection

- Data needs to be assessed from the perspective of the state or Common Core Standards and the grade level expectations. What are the non-negotiables for students to accomplish at that grade level? What can the student do in relation to those expectations?

- What data do you have available to you that provides a summary of student performance in relation to the expectations of the general curriculum?

- Refer back to your state IEP manual handout. What does the manual say you should put here? What do you find now on your current documents?

Related Strengths

- What CAN the student do in RELATION to area of need?

Essential Questions:

- What can the student do?

- What does the student NEED to be able to do?

- What specific academic or behavior skills does the child need in order to be able to perform independently in the classroom?

- What are good data sources? (High Stakes Tests, Curriculum Based Measures and Rubrics—not the Standard Testing from previous years or not related to the standards/curriculum—as appropriate).

- Data needs to be described here – even if age appropriate/consider writing data about strengths that would be useful instructionally.

- Strengths can also be relative (relative to the child's ability—not the grade level expectation).

- Strengths – must be included.

Authentic Identified Need

- What does the student NEED to be able to do?

- What specific academic or behavior skills does the child need in order to be able to perform **independently** in the classroom?

One of the guidelines that will help you to identify an authentic need is to ask yourself, "What does the student need to be able to do right now that if they are unable to do it, then someone else will have to do it for them?"

What skills does the student need to be independent in the classroom either academically or behaviorally?

Prioritize – What does the student need to do right now that he or she cannot do without help?

Is this a delay? Does the student need to catch up?

Is this a compensatory strategy – to compensate for a can't disorder?

Is this an unrealistic expectation?

- What specific skills/strategies does the child need?

- Note the category is concerns/needs and not weaknesses – emphasize "specially designed instruction"

- Define the specially designed instruction

- Stress the connection to goals

Special Education

Defined, as a term of art, in the IDEIA regulations at 34 CFR 300.39(a) ***as specially designed instruction, at no cost to the parents, to meet the unique needs of a child with a disability***, including (a) instruction conducted in the classroom, in the home, in hospitals and institutions, and in other settings; and (b) instruction in physical education.....CFR 300.39(a)(2)(i)-(iii)…"

Keep in mind, we are not in the business of "curing." Is it a delay, a disorder, can it be remediated or do we need to provide student owned strategies?

Reflection

- How do we give a child the skills to learn the curriculum?

Specially Designed Instruction

"Included in the definition of **special education** in Part B regulations at 34 CFR 300.39(b)(3) as ***adapting***, as appropriate to the needs of an eligible **child** under Part B of the IDIEA, the ***content, methodology, or delivery of instruction to address the unique needs of the child that result from the child's disability and to ensure access of the child to the general curriculum***, …"

Reflection

- What does this definition of specially designed instruction mean to you?

- How is "support" different from "specially designed instruction"?

CLEARLY DEFINED Adverse Affect

- Describe **how** the student's disability(ies) affects the student's involvement and progress in the general education curriculum.

- Using data from evaluations establish a direct relationship between the disability condition(s) and adverse affect on education performance.

From IDEA – 300.320(a)(2)(iv) – describe… how the disability affects involvement and progress in the general education curriculum and what the child needs to be involved in and make progress in the general education curriculum.

Impact statement – If there is a concern, what is the impact on participation and progress.

Example: The student's weakness in phonological processing impacts his ability to acquire new vocabulary in content areas without multi-sensory language instruction and accommodations.

Creating the Impact Statement

Rule 300.347 (IDEA): "The IEP for each child must include a statement of the special education and related services and supplementary aides and services to be provided to the child, on behalf of the child, and a statement of the program modifications or supports for school personnel that will be provided for the child (i) to advance appropriately towards attaining the annual goals; (ii) to be involved and progress in the general curriculum in accordance with paragraph (a) (1) of this section."

The purpose for creating an accurate impact statement is that it allows you to create goals and objectives that are more likely to result in educational benefit for the student. In addition, those goals and objectives are more likely to result in the opportunity to pre-plan for the student's participation in the general education setting using research based methods. We want the specially designed instruction to become embedded into the general education setting.

Formula –

1. Identify the specific aspect of the disability.

2. Explain its impact on progress or participation in general education.

3. Describe what is required to ensure student participation in the general education curriculum.

Impact Statement Frame

Due to _____, the student is
(aspect of disability from evaluation data)

unable to _____ without
(grade level expected skill or behavior)

_____
(modifications, accommodations and specially designed instruction)

This was created to give educators a format to write the impact statement and include all of the important information.

Sample Impact Statements

General Example - Due to deficits in executive functioning, Chris is unable to initiate and organize academic tasks without specially designed instruction, accommodations and modifications.

More Specific Example - Due to weaknesses in phonemic awareness and phonological processing, Isabel is unable to decode text at grade level without multisensory reading instruction, accommodations and modifications.

Activity

Read the "more specific" impact statement example. Can you "predict" this child's GOAL areas and possible accommodations and modifications?

Impact Statements – Examples vs. Non-Examples

Academic/ Performance Area	Example	Non-Example
Communication	Due to weaknesses in expressive language, Sarah is unable to communicate ideas and requests to communicative partners without specially designed instruction, accommodations and modifications.	Sarah's poor language skills require special education services.
Communication	Due to deficits in pragmatic language, Doug is unable to participate in small group activities or class discussion in the general education classroom without instruction in pragmatic skills, and scheduling accommodations.	Due to his Autism, Doug cannot participate in the general education setting without special education supports.
Reading/Language Arts	Due to weaknesses in inferential comprehension, Gio is unable to respond to open ended prompts after reading without instruction in reading strategies and accommodations.	Because of a specific learning disability in the area of reading, Gio cannot read and respond to grade level text without special education.
Social/Emotional Behavioral	Due to persistent school phobia, Miguel is unable to attend content area classes regularly to meet course expectations without special instruction in anxiety reducing strategies, and scheduling modifications.	Miguel's SED impact his ability to succeed in school without special education supports.

This is a link to a document that gives examples of what specially designed instruction can look like in different areas. You may want to use this for statement writing practice as a reference. http://www.grrec.ky.gov/CaveWeb/pdf_forms/SDI%20SAS.pdf

Activity

Statement Practice

Use the sample case study and create an impact statement for the academic or performance area below.

CASE STUDY

Niko: Grade 3

AREA

Academic/Cognitive: Language Arts

Niko knows and can apply grade level phonics and word analysis skills when decoding grade level materials. Niko can use the phonics skills in his daily spelling and can clearly write his thoughts. Niko uses his background knowledge when discussing reading topics and has a good vocabulary.

STRENGTHS

With prompting and support, Niko can answer questions about key details in a text. When instructed he will go back into the text and find evidence to support his response. Niko will respond both verbally and in written form to express his understanding of a topic after a lengthy discussion by the group.

CONCERNS/NEEDS

Comprehension

IMPACT STATEMENT

Due to a learning disability in reading, Niko is unable to ask and answer questions to demonstrate his understanding of the text without special education services.

The Blueprint: Building Powerful IEPs to Increase Student Achievement
All Rights Reserved/ www.crec.org

Activity

- Select a PLAAFP from a current IEP.

- Use the Educational Benefit checklist below to analyze how well the PLAAFP is written to result in an IEP that is reasonably calculated to provide Educational Benefit.

- What did you find out?

Activity

Educational Benefit – IEP Checklist

Directions: Review a sample PLAAFP and supporting goals and objectives using the questions below. Use the following questions to reflect on your findings to determine how you may be able to strengthen the PLAAFP.

- Are the concerns of the parent/guardian/student addressed?

- Is the data in each academic/performance area current and present a holistic view of the student's abilities in that area?

- Does the data clearly reflect the student's performance in the educational setting?

- Are the student's strengths clearly identified?

- Does the PLAAFP prioritize the needs identified by the assessment data?

- Does the IEP Team agree on the areas of need to be addressed in goals as identified in the Present Levels of Academic Achievement and Functional Performance?

Goals and Objectives

- Are there goals and objectives/benchmarks (if appropriate) for each area of need and vice versa?

- Are the goals and objectives/benchmarks measurable?

- Do the goals and objectives/benchmarks enable the student to be involved/progress in the general curriculum?

- Is the specially designed instruction identified for each of the objectives/benchmarks? Findings:

- Next Steps/Suggestions:

Educational Benefit Protocol

Ed. Benefit Components	Level 1 = Little Evidence to Indicate Educational Benefit	Level 2 = Some Evidence to Indicate Educational Benefit	Level 3 = Sufficient Evidence to Indicate Educational Benefit
Present Levels of Academic Achievement and Functional Performance	No Data in PLAAFP Irrelevant Data in PLAAFP Area(s) of Need are missing one or more area(s) of strength One or more missing descriptive statements of adverse impact for area(s) of need PLAAFP data is old Data based on general standard scores and not specifics skills	Adequate Data in PLAAFP / Data not interpreted PLAAFP is not data driven Mismatch between areas of need and areas of strength All areas of need do not have a related defined / described adverse impact	Present levels are data driven Data is interpreted in brief summary Data is relevant and recent For each area of need there is a RELATED strength In areas marked as "appropriate" strengths and relative strengths are listed Adverse impact is *clearly* defined for *each* area of need Area(s) of need are directly related to present level data and recent assessment(s), evaluation(s)
Standards Based, Measureable IEP Goals	All IEP goals are NOT *individualized* to student's identified area(s) of need IEP goals are very similar/same as the goals of other students ALL IEP goals are not measureable, data collection methods are not aligned with construct of goal IEP has too many goals and or objectives to implement effectively ALL IEP goals are the same as the previous year's goals IEP goals have not been appropriately marked/graded or updated per IEP	Most of the IEP goals are *individualized* to student's identified area(s) of need The IEP uses a variety of appropriate measurable combinations and not just the combination of "9 G 80%" (in many cases this combination is not measurable) Most of the IEP goals are reflective of the standards, not standards copied Most of the IEP goals are measureable, with effective means of measurement Most of IEP goals are different from the previous year's goals	ALL IEP goals are *individualized* to student's identified area(s) of need, with appropriate and varying measurability ALL IEP goals are standards based ALL IEP goals are measureable, with effective means of measurement ALL IEP goals have at least two measureable objectives ALL IEP goals are different from the previous year's goals Given the student's PLAAFP, there are an appropriate number of IEP goals/objectives than can be effectively implemented and reached in a 12 month period.

Accommodations and Modifications	No connection between accommodations and or modifications, given the student's learning profile as described in the PLAAFP	Minimal amount of connection between the Accommodations and Modifications listed, given the student's learning profile as described in PLAAFP	Accommodations and Modifications listed are aligned to student's learning profile as described in PLAAFP
Service Time	Amount of service time for each IEP goal is inappropriate given the relationship between the needs of the area of deficit(s) and the IEP goals	Amount of service time for each IEP goal is questionable given the relationship between the needs of the area of deficit(s) and the IEP goals	Service time for each IEP goal is appropriate given the relationship between the needs of the area of deficit(s) and the IEP goals

Extended Activity

You can go further with this activity if they can access three consecutive years of IEPs for one student.

- Has the student made progress from one year to the next?

- Have the goals and objectives been mastered?

- Have the goals and objectives changed from year to year?

Activity

Directions: Rewrite the PLAAFP for the sample IEP OR

Rewrite the PLAAFP for a student IEP on your caseload

Present Level of Academic and Functional Performance – Sample/Example

PRESENT LEVELS OF ACADEMIC ACHIEVEMENT AND FUNCTIONAL PERFORMANCE
(The following information was derived from: report data, documentation from classroom performance, parent /student reports, curriculum based and standardized assessments, observations, including CMT and CAPT results and student samples).

Parent and Student input and concerns _____ is concerned about the reported behaviors from school and noted that she reinforces with him at home that he needs to listen to teachers and follow directions even if he doesn't like what they are saying.

Area (briefly describe current performance)	Strengths (include data as appropriate)	Concerns/Needs (requiring specialized instruction)	Impact of student's disability on involvement and progress in the general education curriculum or appropriate preschool activities.
Academic/Cognitive: Language Arts: ☐ Age Appropriate F&P level H 12/2012-can ask questions, uses pictures to make meaning, Benchmark Writing 17/36; Universal Screens-high risk, Reading Test average 79%; ORF 32 wpm; Dolch Sight Words 1-40/40;	Bryson shows a general excitement for learning and in his own accomplishments. He can be a diligent hard working student and is very personable. Bryson has a good fund of vocabulary words, spells grade level words correctly on weekly tests and answers comprehension questions with picture supports.	Bryson has a lack of confidence in his ability and often waits for an indication that he is correct before he will continue working on his own. He does not automatically apply the rules he has learned to decoding when reading and has trouble with inferential comprehension.	Due to weaknesses in self-monitoring, Bryson is unable to answer inferential questions about grade level text without a multi-component reading intervention, accommodations and modifications.
Academic/Cognitive: Math: ☐ Age Appropriate Universal Math screen fall 2012 - 0, Bryson has mastered 1:1 correspondence to 20. He can sort, group and classify items.	Bryson has mastered 1:1 correspondence to 20. He can sort, group and classify items.	Bryson still struggles with number sense, 1:1 correspondence past 20 objects, equal to, greater than and less than concepts; math facts +1	Due to weaknesses in working memory and attention, Bryson is unable to apply grade level math strategies and skills without a multi-component math intervention program, environmental and academic accommodations.
Other Academic/Nonacademic Areas: ☐ Age Appropriate			

PRESENT LEVELS OF ACADEMIC ACHIEVEMENT AND FUNCTIONAL PERFORMANCE

Area (briefly describe current performance)	Strengths (include data as appropriate)	Concerns/Needs (requiring specialized instruction)	Impact of student's disability on involvement and progress in the general education curriculum or appropriate preschool activities.
Behavioral/Social/Emotional: ☐ Age Appropriate Bryson currently follows a Behavior Intervention Plan that includes a daily tracking chart.	Bryson is kind and considerate to other students when he is calm. He enjoys social interactions, greets familiar adults with enthusiasm, loves adult attention, often compliment others and offers to help.	Bryson struggles with turn taking, talking out, keeping hands feet and mouth to self when angry and participating in group lessons at the carpet. Bryson struggles first thing in the morning with keeping his body in control and safe.	Due to weaknesses in executive functions, Bryson is unable to maintain and shift attention during non-preferred activities without positive behavioral supports, accommodations and modifications.
Communication: ☐ Age Appropriate Bryson is able to engage in conversations. He has made progress in answering simple "Why and When" questions.	Bryson has a good fund of vocabulary words and can answer 'why and when' questions with picture support.	Bryson struggles to answer 'who and what' comprehension questions, understand quantity concepts, has below grade level knowledge of word relationships (synonyms and antonyms).	Delays in receptive language skills impact Bryson's ability to comprehend grade level material without accommodations & specially designed instruction. Weakness with quantitative concepts impact his ability to comprehend grade level math without accommodations & specially designed instruction.
Vocational/Transition: ☑ Age Appropriate			
Health and Development-Including Vision and Hearing: ☑ Age Appropriate Diagnosis and treatment for ADHD			This is the student's primary disability.
Fine and Gross Motor: ☑ Age Appropriate Difficulties with pace of written work is not due to fine motor or visual perceptual skills. Bryson has difficulties completing tactile experiences (art and science).	Hard worker	Physical therapy screen is recommended to observe midline crossing difficulties.	
Activities of Daily Living: ☑ Age Appropriate			
Other: ☐ Age Appropriate			

Closing: Review of Key Ideas

Selecting relevant sources of data to determine a student's present level of performance is essential in constructing an educational program that will provide educational benefit.

Parental input is critical in determining a student's present levels of performance.

Identifying the impact of the student's disability on progress in the general curriculum leads to appropriate goals and objectives.

Key Quote

"We must not, in trying to think about how we can make a big difference, ignore the small daily differences we can make which, over time, add up to big differences that we often cannot foresee."
– MARIAN WRIGHT EDELMAN

By attending to the small details of the PLAAFP, we can make a big difference in a child's IEP.

Reflections to Inform Your Practice

1. Summarize the important aspects of writing an accurate and viable PLAAFP.

2. What practices am I going to apply in my job or what experiences will I try?

3. What did I try and did it work? Why or why not?

4. What will I try next?

Assess Your Learning

Module 1 – Defining Present Levels of Academic Achievement and Functional Performance (PLAAFP)

1. How many concerns should be listed in any one academic/performance area?

2. Can the same impact statement be used in more than one academic/performance area?

3. Do you have to specifically describe the type of specially designed instruction that will address your concerns in the impact statement?

Answers to Assess Your Learning

Module 1 – Defining Present Levels of Academic Achievement and Functional Performance (PLAAFP)

1. **How many concerns should be listed in any one academic/performance area?**

   There is no set number of concerns for each area. However, the student performance data should be used to prioritize concerns or needs. Students who receive special education services often have many areas of weakness as a result of the impact of their disability on their academic achievement and performance. Special educators and related service personnel should consider what can reasonably be accomplished during the term of the IEP. The IEP should develop goals (and in some cases objectives) that can be mastered in the 12 month period of that year's IEP. Also, IEP teams need to ask what concerns can be addressed that would have the greatest impact in increasing student achievement and access to the curriculum.

2. **Can the same impact statement be used in more than one academic/performance area?**

   The impact statement should identify the *aspect* of the disability that influences student achievement and performance in the curriculum. So, ideally, the impact statement should not be the same in each academic/performance area.

3. **Do you have to specifically describe the type of specially designed instruction that will address your concerns in the impact statement?**

   IDEA Sec. 300.320(a)(1)(i) states that the PLAAFP must describe "how the disability affects involvement and progress in general education and what the child needs to be involved in and make progress in the general education curriculum." The special services support team recommends identifying methodology that enables the child to access the general education curriculum. See examples of impact statements in Handouts.

Building Powerful IEPs to Increase Student Achievement

Module 2:

Writing Standards-Based Individual Education Plans (IEPs)

In this Module you will

- ✓ Understand why standards-based IEPs are important

- ✓ Learn the characteristics of an effective standards-based IEP

- ✓ Practice strategies to make the IEP is measurable

- ✓ Create IEPs that can be evaluated

- ✓ Identify methods of data collection

Module 2 Writing Standards-Based Individual Education Plans

The temptation to form premature theories upon insufficient data is the bane of our profession.
-SHERLOCK HOLMES

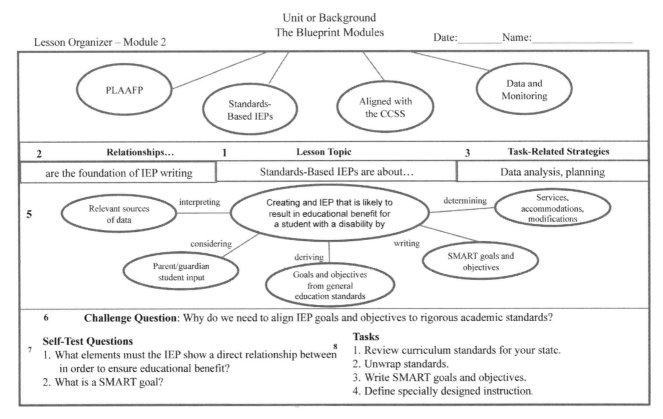

Lesson Organizer – Module 2

Unit or Background
The Blueprint Modules

Date:_____ Name:_____

PLAAFP

Standards-Based IEPs

Aligned with the CCSS

Data and Monitoring

2	Relationships...	1	Lesson Topic	3	Task-Related Strategies
	are the foundation of IEP writing		Standards-Based IEPs are about...		Data analysis, planning

5

Relevant sources of data

interpreting

Creating and IEP that is likely to result in educational benefit for a student with a disability by

determining

Services, accommodations, modifications

considering

writing

Parent/guardian student input

deriving

SMART goals and objectives

Goals and objectives from general education standards

6   **Challenge Question**: Why do we need to align IEP goals and objectives to rigorous academic standards?

Self-Test Questions

7
1. What elements must the IEP show a direct relationship between in order to ensure educational benefit?
2. What is a SMART goal?

8

Tasks
1. Review curriculum standards for your state.
2. Unwrap standards.
3. Write SMART goals and objectives.
4. Define specially designed instruction.

Questions I Hope Get Answered

What are the questions or concerns you have about the Standards-Based IEPs that you hope will be addressed?

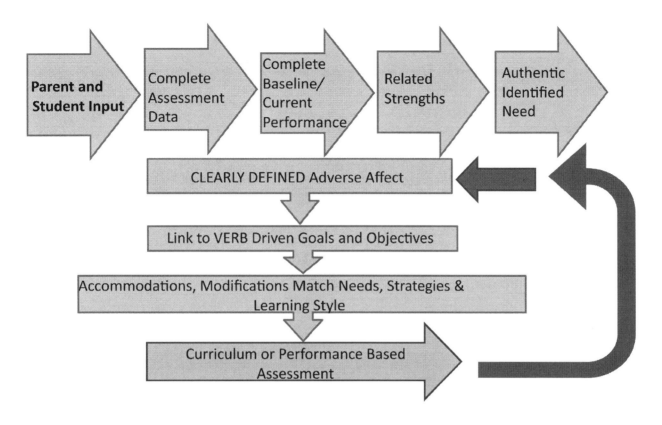

This graphic represents the educational benefit process as discussed in Module 1. The educational benefit process begins with well informed IEPs (parent and student input, assessment and current performance data, identified need). This leads to clearly define how the disability adversely affects educational performance. Goals are written with clear action verbs and measurable outcomes. After goals are determined, THEN modifications are considered. Finally, assessment and outcomes and services are calculated based on the information.

Reflection

- What is the purpose of the IEP?

- How often does it drive what you do with the student in a special education classroom?

- In a general education classroom?

- Is there ever a disconnect? If so, why?

The IEP meeting serves as a communication vehicle between parents and school personnel. It enables them, as equal participants, to jointly decide what the child's needs are, what services will be provided to meet those needs, and what the anticipated outcomes may be.

The IEP process provides an opportunity for resolving any differences between the parents and the agency concerning the special education needs of a child with a disability. The IEP meeting is the first step and, if necessary, the procedural protections that are available to the parents can be a next step.

The IEP sets forth in writing a commitment of resources necessary to enable a child with a disability to receive the necessary special education and related services.

Parents as Equals
- Rights to participate in a meeting

- Meeting communication barriers

- Talk about standards

Reflection

- What are some ways that you involve parents in the IEP process?

- How can you make parents feel like they are a member of the team?

The Blueprint: Building Powerful IEPs to Increase Student Achievement
All Rights Reserved/ www.crec.org

- How does parent participation add to or subtract from services?

Characteristics of a Standards-Based IEP

- Assessment data is clearly outlined

- Statements of current educational performance relate to district standards

- Strengths and needs relate to the academic content and access skills

- Goals/objectives address the critical academic content and access skills

- Goals/objectives are strategic, measurable, attainable, results-driven, and time-bound (SMART)

- Measurements of progress include descriptions of classroom/district assessments, individualized, applied performance demonstrations

Seven Step Process

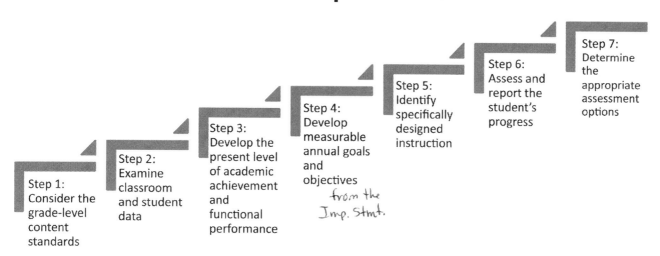

Step 1: Consider the grade-level content standards

Step 2: Examine classroom and student data

Step 3: Develop the present level of academic achievement and functional performance

Step 4: Develop measurable annual goals and objectives *from the Imp. Stmt.*

Step 5: Identify specifically designed instruction

Step 6: Assess and report the student's progress

Step 7: Determine the appropriate assessment options

Step One

Consider the grade-level content standards for the grade in which the student is enrolled or would be enrolled based on age.

It is important that educators frequently visit and review these standards when considering educational programming for students with disabilities.

Activity

Directions: Download the Common Core Standards at www.corestandards.org

Please review the Common Core standards in a particular area for a grade that you teach.

- What is the intent of the standard?

CCSS.ELA- LITERACY.RI, 9-10.1

(Cite) strong and thorough textual evidence to (support) analysis of what the text says explicitly as well as inferences drawn from the text.

- What do the standards say that the student must know and be able to do?

- Are there patterns that emerge in the language used in the standards that need special emphasis for instruction? For example, the Common Core Standards emphasize oral language skills, metacognition, and collaboration skills in all areas.

- What is the essence of the standard to consider for the child that is functioning significantly below grade level? For example, a student in the fifth grade needs to identify the components of a complex narrative and use them in their writing. (5.W.3) Could a student with a significant disability sequence the steps of a multi-step activity? The link for this student's needs to the grade level standard is sequencing skills.

Be able to state evidence about why you know what you know.

Unwrap the Standards and Unlock the Goals

- Underline the nouns (the concepts) and the noun phrases

- Circle the verbs

- Nouns = concepts

- Verbs = skills

Example: Use combined knowledge of all letter-sound correspondences, syllabication patterns, and morphology (e.g., roots and affixes) to read accurately unfamiliar multisyllabic words in context and out of context.

Skills and Concept T-Chart

Skills	Concepts
Read unfamiliar multisyllabic words in and out of context	• letter sound correspondences • syllabication patterns • morphology

Reflection

- What other tools exist in your state that can help you to determine the essence of the Common Core Standards?

- Can those tools also assist you to determine appropriate instructional entry points at lower levels of complexity based on your student's present level of performance?

Step Two

Examine classroom and student data to determine where the student is functioning in relation to the grade-level standards.

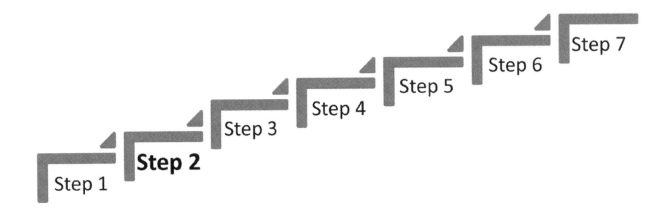

Reflection

- Has the student been taught content aligned with grade-level standards?

- Has the student been provided appropriate instructional scaffolding to attain grade-level expectations?

- Were the lessons and teaching materials used to teach the student aligned with state grade-level standards?

- Was the instruction evidence-based?

- What supports and services worked in the past?

- What goals has the student mastered? How was that accomplished?

Step Three

Develop the present level of academic achievement and functional performance.

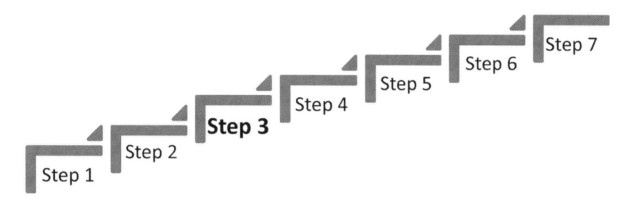

Reflection

- What do we know about the student's response to academic instruction (e.g. progress monitoring data)?

- What programs, accommodations (i.e. classroom and testing) and/or interventions have been successful with the student?

- What have we learned from previous IEPs and student data that can inform decision making?

- Is there assessment data (i.e. state, district and/or classroom) that can provide useful information for making decisions about the student's strengths and needs?

Step Four

Develop measurable annual goals and objectives aligned with grade-level academic content standards.

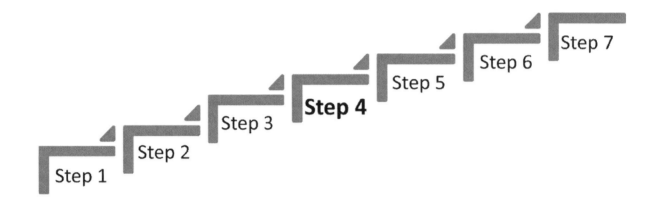

Reflection

- What are the student's needs as identified in the present level of performance?

- Does the goal have a specific timeframe?

- What can the student reasonably be expected to accomplish in one school year?

- Are the conditions for meeting the goal addressed?

- How will the outcome of the goal be measured?

Measurable Annual Goals

- Statements that describe what we expect a child to accomplish within a 12 month period.

- A goal must include an observable learner performance, specify the criterion or level of satisfactory performance and include any essential givens or conditions.

Activity

Determine:

- What are the parts of a measurable goal?

- Does the quality of the parts matter?

Sample Goal: The volunteer will assemble balloons with 80% accuracy as measured by group observation of a daily one minute trial.

Measurability

- "Measurable" means you can count it or observe it.

- Appropriate question: "What do I see the student doing that makes me make the above judgment call?"

- What you actually see the student doing is the measurable content you need to identify in your present level.

A well-written goal uses objective language that clearly describes what the student will do under certain circumstances.

Measurability – Degree of Mastery

- Specify a grade or age level performance, if definable through district standards or other curriculum or through known scope and sequence materials, developmental materials, or through testing materials.

- Indicate rate, frequency, speed, distance, number of trials, and by date.

For example: 3 out of 4 times, 80% of the time, 5 minutes out of every 10, 75% success. Be cautious when using grade level performance. Grade level expectations can vary from district to district especially with regard to grades.

Measurability – Conditions

You can make student behavior measurable by:

1. defining the factors surrounding the behavior.

These include:

- ✓ precipitating events

- ✓ environmental factors

2. identifying the results of the behavior.

Examples of precipitating events – "when asked to work independently."

Examples of environmental factors – "when being directed by female authority figures," "after lunch," "in math class," "on the playground."

Examples of identifying the results of the behavior – "removal from the classroom has increased this behavior."

Goals

"Goals and objectives should be specific, measurable and, **to the extent appropriate**, relate the student's achievement in the general education curriculum;" CT SDE IEP Manual p. 12.

Sample Goal

To remain on task for at least 10 minutes during a teacher-directed desktop assignment or activity, with no ~~less~~ *more* than two verbal prompts in three out of four trials as measured by data collection charts. Educational Advocates, "Breaking Down the IEP: Measurable Annual Goals," July 22, 2009

Critical Questions for Goal Writing (*Wrightslaw: All About IEPs, 2010*)

- What is the problem that you hope to address?

- Is this an increase or a decrease? *(do not use the word improve)*

- What is the present level? *under 10*

- What level of mastery does that the team expect? *at least 10*

- How will mastery be measured? *3 out of 4 trials with no more than two verbal prompts*

Reflection

- If a child has the same goal for more than one year, has the IEP been calculated for the child to derive educational benefit?

Specific
Measurable
Attainable
Realistic
Timely

Sample Goal

The components of the goal includes the problem that you seek to address, the amount of change, the present level of performance and the mastery measurement.

- Problem – number of correct writing sequences in written work

- Increase or decrease – increase to 75 correct sequences in 100 words

- Present level – 55 correct sequences in 100 written words

- Mastery – three consecutive writing probes

- Measurement – curriculum based measurement

Complete Goal

The student will increase the number of correct writing sequences from 55 correct sequences in 100 words to 75 correct sequences in 100 words in three consecutive writing probes.

From CC Standard Four, Grade 5 Production and Distribution of Writing - Produce clear and coherent writing in which the development and organization are appropriate to task, purpose, and audience.

The SMART Goal Connection

- ✓ Specific – increase the number of correct writing sequences

- ✓ Measurable – 75 correct writing sequences in 100 words

- ✓ Achievable – 55 to 75 correct writing sequences in 12 months

- ✓ Relevant – CCS 5.W.4

- ✓ Time bound – the term of the IEP

- ✓ Objectives that could accompany this goal:

  - Given direct instruction in a sentence writing strategy, the student will use three different conjunctions (and, but, or), to combine sentences with 80% accuracy in three consecutive writing samples.

  - Given direct instruction in "chunking," the student will correctly spell multi-syllabic words with 80% accuracy in three consecutive writing samples.

  - Given an editing strategy, the student will use correct capitalization at the beginning of a sentence, proper nouns, and the first word in a quotation with 85% accuracy in three consecutive writing samples.

Directions: Rewrite this goal to be more specific, measurable, achievable, relevant and time bound (SMART). Old Goal: Sarah will improve written language. Refer back to Critical Questions for Goal Writing.

Base your goal on the grade level you are currently working.

Example: Sarah will write a five sentence paragraph with a topic sentence, three detail sentences and a summary statement with fewer than three grammatical errors to increase score on district writing rubric from four to six out of 10 in four of five writing prompt samples.

Objectives

Some states do not use objectives, but if your state does, here are some things you should know:

Objectives should include:

- the specially designed instruction

- the target behavior or skill

- the conditions under which the student will demonstrate mastery

- the level of mastery expected

Short-Term Objectives

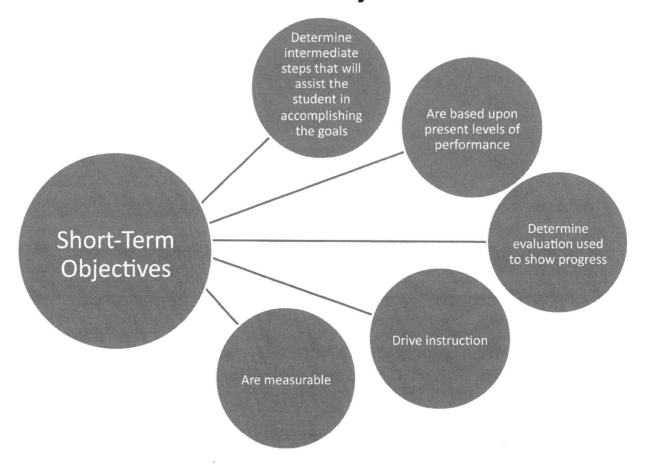

Objectives can be written either as a scope and sequence of activities that will enable the student to accomplish the goal or as instructional statements about the strategies that the student will be taught to allow him/her to master the goal.

Short-Term Objectives

Example: Given prediction and summarization strategies, X will be able to state the main idea and two details of a grade level selection under 300 words independently with 100% accuracy in three consecutive attempts. (CCS, Grade 6, Informational Text, 2)

Example: Given direct instruction in "guess and check" and "make a chart," X will independently apply strategies to solve five word problems with at least 80% accuracy in three consecutive attempts. (CCS, Grade 4, Operations and Algebraic Thinking, 3)

Step Five

Identify specially designed instruction including accommodations and/or modifications needed to access and progress in the general education curriculum.

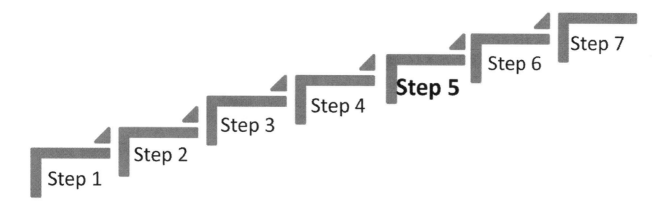

Reflection

- What accommodations are needed to enable the student to access the knowledge in the general education curriculum?

- What accommodations have been used with the student and were they effective?

- Has the complexity of the material been changed in such a way that the content or curriculum expectation has been modified?

- Does the student need specially designed instruction to access the standards?

- What new skill would immediately make the child a more successful, independent learner?

Special Education

"Defined, as a term of art, in the IDEA regulations at 34 CFR 300.39(a) *as **specially designed instruction, at no cost to the parents, to meet the unique needs of a child with a disability,*** including (a) instruction conducted in the classroom, in the home, in hospitals and institutions, and in other settings; and (b) instruction in **physical education**.....CFR 300.39(a)(2)(i)-(iii). …"

Keep in mind that we are not in the business of "curing." Is it a delay or a disorder? Can it be remediated or do we need to provide student owned strategies?

Specially Designed Instruction

"Included in the definition of **special education** in Part B regulations at 34 CFR 300.39(b)(3) as ***adapting***, as appropriate to the needs of an eligible **child** under Part B of the IDEA, the ***content, methodology, or delivery of instruction to address the unique needs of the child that result from the child's disability and to ensure access of the child to the general curriculum***, …"

Reflection

- Note the bolded words. What is the difference between specially designed instruction, modifications, and accommodations?

Step Five

- What will the child learn to do that is DIFFERENT from the general expectations?

- Adaptations may be placed on modification page. What materials and supports will the child need to function as independently as possible?

Step Six

Assess and reports the students progress throughout the year.

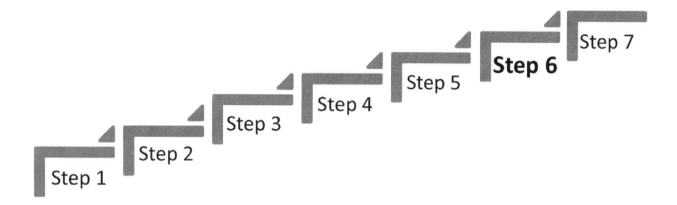

Reflection

- How will progress be reported to parents?

- How will data be collected? What progress monitoring procedures will you use to collect, chart, and reflect on the data?

Step Seven

Determine the most appropriate assessment option.

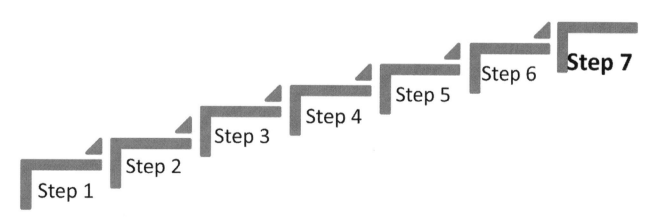

Reflection

- How does the student demonstrate what he/she knows on classroom, district and state assessments?

- Are there a variety of assessments used to measure progress?

- How will progress be reported to parents?

- How will data be collected? What progress monitoring procedures will you use to collect, chart, and reflect on the data?

Measuring and Reporting Progress

- Identify tools to be used **before, during, and after instruction.**

- Keep parents informed about their child's progress at least as often as parents of children who do not have disabilities.

- If a student is not making progress a PPT should be held to review the IEP.

The goal is to transform data into information, and information into insight.

- CARLY FIORINA
EXECUTIVE AND PRESIDENT OF
HEWLETT-PACKARD CO., 1999

Reflections to Inform Your Practice

1. Summarize the important aspects of writing standards based goals and objectives.

2. What practices am I going to apply in my job or what experiences will I try?

3. What did I try and did it work why or why not?

4. What will I try next?

Assess Your Learning

Module 2 – Standards-Based Goals and Objectives

1. Is there a there a specific number of goals (and if required, objectives) that should be in an IEP?

2. Should the program being used with the student be named in the goals or objectives?

3. Will an IEP have more goals and objectives if they are written in a more specific manner?

Answers to Assess Your Learning

Module 2 – Standards-Based Goals and Objectives

1. **Is there a there a specific number of goals (and if required, objectives) that should be in an IEP?**

   There is no limit on the number of goals that can be included in the IEP. Federal Reg., Section 300.347(a)(2) requires that each child's IEP include: "A statement of measurable annual goals, including benchmarks or short-term objectives, related to(i) meeting the child's needs that result from the child's disability to enable the child to be involved in and progress in the general curriculum ...; and(ii) meeting each of the child's other educational needs that result from the child's disability....". In addition, the June 2007 NASDE Project Forum on Standards-Based IEPs states that the goals should be those that can reasonably be accomplished in one year's time. It is up to the team to determine what can realistically be mastered during the term of the IEP.

2. **Should the program being used with the student be named in the goals or objectives?**

   No. Names of specific programs should not be included with the goals or objectives. However, it is appropriate to refer to methods that will be used to provide specially designed instruction. For example, teachers can refer to the use of multi-sensory instruction, task analysis, least to most prompts, etc. to describe the techniques that will be used to meet student goals and objectives.

3. **Will an IEP have more goals and objectives if they are written in a more specific manner?**

   No. The IEP is intended to be a minimal document. This training is designed to help teachers and related service personnel target student needs that rise to the level of requiring specially designed instruction. The goal is to provide services in those areas that will have the greatest impact on the student's independence and success within the term of that IEP. Students with disabilities have many needs. The purpose of the IEP is to design instruction for that school year that will accelerate that student's participation and success in the general education setting.

Building Powerful IEPs to Increase Student Achievement

Module 3

Creating Instruction from the Common Core Standards for Special Education and Related Services

In this Module you will

- ✓ Understand the organization of the CCS

- ✓ Identify changes in the focus of instruction for ELA and Math

- ✓ Define critical skills for success in the CCS for educational benefit

- ✓ Analyze instructional approaches and tools for creating specially designed instruction

Module 3 Creating Instruction from the Common Core Standards and Related Services

Education is not the piling on of learning, information, data, facts, skills, or abilities - that's training or instruction - but is rather making visible what is hidden as a seed.

— THOMAS MOORE

This quote represents the key ideas of Module 3:

- Use of a carefully designed IEP

- The importance of IEP data

- Knowing information about the student

In order to reveal instruction that will grow a student's social and academic abilities.

Questions I Hope Get Answered

What are the questions or concerns you have about Common Core Standards and the IEP that you hope will be addressed?

Common Core Standards (CCS)

Video Activity:

This video is part of an extensive series of videos from the Hunt Institute on the CCS and the important information that educators need to know to implement the standards in their classroom. Please go to http://www.youtube.com/watch?v=d1MVErnOD7c and watch the video.

Use the Video Viewing Guide below and answer the questions during or after the video.

Hunt Institute Video Viewing Guide

1. What are the five principles behind the Common Core Standards?

    1.

    2.

    3

    4.

    5.

2. How many states have adopted the Common Core Standards?

3. How does the Common Core Standards create students who are college and career ready?

4. What evidence was used to develop the Common Core Standards?

5. Why is the idea of **focus** so important to improve academic success for students?

6. Do the Common Core Standards tell states how they must teach for students to master the standards? Why or why not?

Activity: A Closer Look

We have provided you with four videos to review. Each one of these videos gives you an opportunity to review and preview information related to the CCS. You can scan the QR code or use the website we have provided.

Use the summary graphic organizer to help you gather the information from the videos.

1. "ELA Standards – Key Changes and Their Evidence" by The Hunt Institute –

   Discusses the instructional shifts in the CCS ELA standards.

   http://www.youtube.com/watch?v=JDzTOyxRGLI

2. "Three Minute Video Explaining the CCSS" by dcpublicschools

   This is an engaging overview of the CCS and how it prepares students to be college and career ready. http://www.youtube.com/watch?v=5s0rRk9sER0

3. "The Mathematics Standards: Key Changes and Their Evidence" by The Hunt Institute

   This video reviews the instructional shifts of the CCS Math standards.

   http://www.youtube.com/watch?v=BNP5MdDDFPY

4. "CCSS and Special Education" by Don Johnston

   This is a nice overview of the CCS and how it will impact special education.

   http://www.youtube.com/watch?v=0Uv1DfFaahU

Summary Graphic Organizer

3	Things I Learned Today …
2	Things I Found Interesting …
1	Question I Still Have …

Unwrapping the CCS

Skills (verbs)	Concepts (nouns, noun phrases)		Criteria for Proficient Performance (modifiers)
Report	Text	Main Idea	Logically
Present	Topic	Details	Appropiate
Speak	Opinion	Themes	Relevant
Sequence	Ideas		Descriptive
State			Clearly
			Understandable

The original standard for Unwrapping the CCS is: "Report on a topic or text or present an opinion, sequencing ideas logically and using appropriate facts and relevant, descriptive details to support main ideas or themes; speak clearly at an understandable pace." (Common Core Standards English Language Arts Speaking and Listening, Grade 5, Number 4)

The purpose for unwrapping a standard is to identify precisely what the students must know and be able to do in order to master the standard. The verbs represent the skills, or what the student must do to meet the standards. The nouns and noun phrases represent the concepts that the student must know in order to perform the skills needed to master the standard.

In order to unwrap the standards, you will need to underline the nouns and noun phrases and circle the verbs. You should also make note of the adverbs and adjectives that describe the criteria for mastery of the standards.

Activity

Directions: Select a standard from the English Language Arts or Math. Use the 3T Chart and Depth of Knowledge chart and transfer the information from the standard into the appropriate sections on the 3T Chart.

3T Chart

Skills (Verbs)	Concepts (Nouns, Noun Phrases)	Criteria for Proficient Performance (Modifiers)

Reflection

- What kind of instruction will you need to design for your students with disabilities to access and acquire the skills and concepts in these standards?

- What did you find?

Depth of Knowledge (DOK) Levels

Level One Activities	Level Two Activities	Level Three Activities	Level Four Activities
Recall elements and details of story structure, such as sequence of events, character, plot and setting.	Identify and summarize the major events in a narrative.	Support ideas with details and examples.	Conduct a project that requires specifying a problem, designing and conducting an experiment, analyzing its data, and reporting results/ solutions.
Conduct basic mathematical calculations.	Use context cues to identify the meaning of unfamiliar words.	Use voice appropriate to the purpose and audience.	Apply mathematical model to illuminate a problem or situation.
Label locations on a map.	Solve routine multiple-step problems.	Identify research questions and design investigations for a scientific problem.	Analyze and synthesize information from multiple sources.
Represent in words or diagrams a scientific concept or relationship.	Describe the cause/effect of a particular event.	Develop a scientific model for a complex situation.	Describe and illustrate how common themes are found across texts from different cultures.
Perform routine procedures like measuring length or using punctuation marks correctly.	Identify patterns in events or behavior.	Determine the author's purpose and describe how it affects the interpretation of a reading selection.	Design a mathematical model to inform and solve a practical or abstract situation.
Describe the features of a place or people.	Formulate a routine problem given data and conditions.	Apply a concept in other contexts.	
	Organize, represent and interpret data.		

Webb, Norman L. and others. "Web Alignment Tool" 24 July 2005. Wisconsin Center of Educational Research. University of Wisconsin-Madison. 2 Feb. 2006. <http://www.wcer.wisc.edu/WAT/index.aspx>.

Instructional Shifts – ELA

- Balanced literary and informational text – a greater balance of informational and literary text is read by students.

- Disciplinary literacy – students build knowledge about content through text rather than by teacher led activities.

- Staircase of complexity – students read a central, grade appropriate text through which instruction is centered and the teacher guides students through opportunities for close reading.

- Text based answers – Students engage in rich, evidence based conversations about text.

- Writing from sources – Writing emphasizes use of evidence from sources to inform or make an argument.

- Academic vocabulary – Students constantly build the transferable vocabulary the need to access grade level complex texts.

Instructional Shifts – Math

- Focus – Teachers significantly narrow and deepen the scope of how time and energy is spent in the math classroom. They do so in order to focus deeply on only the concepts that are prioritized in the standards.

- Coherence – Principals and teachers carefully connect the learning within and across grades so that students can build new understanding onto foundations built in previous years.

- Fluency – Students are expected to have speed and accuracy with simple calculations; and teachers structure class time and/or homework time for students to memorize, through repetition, core functions.

- Deep Understanding – Students deeply understand and can operate easily within a math concept before moving on. They learn more than the trick to get the answer right. They learn the math.

- Application – Students are expected to use math and choose the appropriate concept for application even when they are not prompted to do so.

- Dual Intensity – Students are practicing and understanding. There is more than a balance between these two things in the classroom – both are occurring with intensity.

Activity

Directions: Review the CCS Math Standards for Practice on www.corestandards.org or on the MasteryConnect Common Core app on a tablet or a smart phone.

What stands out for you in relation to the students that you are currently working with?

What impact might this have on how you write math goals and objectives?

How do we develop the necessary perseverance, flexibility, language, and reasoning skills that will enable students with disabilities to master the math standards?

Note:

Developing an accurate representation of the student through the Present Level of Academic and Functional Performance (PLAAFP) in relation to the grade level standards is important so appropriate instruction can be designed that will make achievement of those standards as accessible as possible.

CCS and Student Success

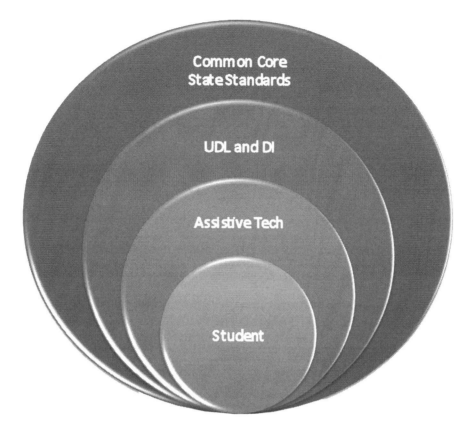

This graphic is used to represent the supports and strategies that will be necessary for students to have success with the CCS.

Assistive Tech = Assistive Technology (AT) is a generic term that includes assistive, adaptive, and rehabilitative devices for people with disabilities.

UDL = Universal Design for Learning is an educational framework based on research in the learning sciences, including cognitive neuroscience, that guides the development of flexible learning environments that can accommodate individual learning differences.

DI = Differentiated Instruction is a framework or philosophy for effective teaching that involves providing students **with different avenues to acquiring content; to processing, constructing, or making sense of** ideas; **and to developing** teaching materials **and assessment measures so that all students within a** classroom **can** learn **effectively, regardless of differences in ability.**

Overarching Shifts for Individual Programs

Learning builds over time
Application of knowledge and skills
Active participation and interaction
Collaboration and communication
Comprehensive instruction

The shifts described above are very important. 57% of students with disabilities spend more than 80% of their day in general education classrooms, yet general education teachers report that they do not have the skills they need to effectively instruct diverse learners, including students with disabilities.

Source for Statistic: Blanton, L. , Pugach, C., Florian, L. (2011), Preparing general education teachers to improve outcomes for students with disabilities. (policy number not given). AACTE Policy Brief, May 9, 2011

Learning Builds Over Time

The CCS are written in learning progressions. These learning progressions "describe a sequence of increasing sophistication in understanding and skill within an area of study." Bradford Findell, April 15, 2011, NCTM Annual Meeting

There are three types of progressions:

1. Learning progressions

2. Standards progressions

3. Task progressions

For example, ELA Standard Reading Literature 3 requires students to describe a character in 3rd grade, describe a character in depth in 4th grade and compare two or more characters in a story in 5th grade. This has particular bearing for students with disabilities because it reminds us that there is a developmental course for skill development. We need to accurately describe what students with disabilities know and can do so we can identify the appropriate instructional entry points according to those grade level standards. This way we can make sure that students can participate appropriately in grade level instruction and acquire skills necessary for long term success in any academic area. Also, by understanding the sequence of skill development, we can prevent the development of scattered skills in any area.

Activity

Select one standard from the CCS Progression Chart below and be able to describe the change in complexity for three grade levels.

CCS Progression Chart

CCS Standard Write Standard Here	Grade	Grade	Grade

Application of Knowledge and Skills

Reflection

- What does application of knowledge and skills mean to you?

Active Participation and Interaction

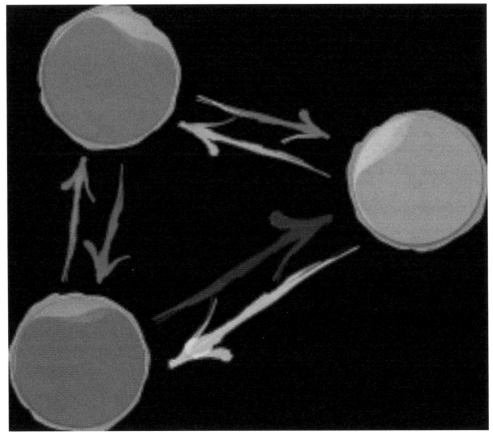

Reflection

- What does active participation and interaction mean to you?

Collaboration and Communication

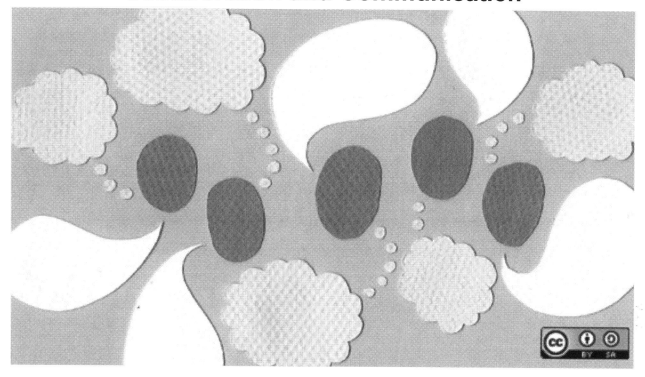

Reflection

- Take a look at the CCS. How many standards use the words describe, explain, discuss, justify, speak, present, engage, argue, construct, critique?

- How often do we create specially designed instruction that is intended to develop these skills?

- Can you describe what the specially designed instruction would look like that helps students to build the skills necessary to communicate and collaborate?

Comprehensive Instruction

Instruction should follow a developmental course and result in the acquisition of skills that students need to be successful in school and everyday life.

Specially Designed Instruction

"Included in the definition of **special education** in Part B regulations at 34 CFR 300.39(b)(3) as ***adapting***, as appropriate to the needs of an eligible **child** under Part B of the IDEA, the ***content, methodology, or delivery of instruction to address the unique needs of the child that result from the child's disability and to ensure access of the child to the general curriculum***,…"

Note the bolded words. This legal definition of specially education is characterized by the specially designed instruction that we provide to students with disabilities.

Source: IDEIA 2004

The three components of specially designed instruction should be considered and/or addressed when developing instruction for a student with disabilities.

How do we adapt:

- content

- methodology

- delivery of instruction at the point of instruction

Unwrapping the CCS

Skills (verbs)	Concepts (nouns, noun phrases)		Criteria for Proficient Performance (modifiers)
Report	Text	Main Idea	Logically
Present	Topic	Details	Appropiate
Speak	Opinion	Themes	Relevant
Sequence	Ideas		Descriptive
State			Clearly
			Understandable

This graphic helps you to make the connection between what the students need to know and be able to do to meet this standard and the specially designed instruction may be needed by students with disabilities to access and achieve the standards.

For example, the verbs in this standard imply proficiency in oral and written language. What specially designed instruction or underlying skills might students need to master in order to access and achieve this standard?

Reflection

- What targeted interventions or personalized learning supports might students need to identify main idea and supporting details?

- What social/emotional and behavioral skills will students need to meet the criteria for proficient performance?

- What skills do we teach through specially designed instruction?

- Look back at the standard that you unwrapped.

- Refer to the graphic organizer and brainstorm a list of skills that may require specially designed instruction in each area that we will need to teach in each of the organizer headings.

Activity

The purpose of this activity is for you to take a closer look at the standards that you unwrapped in the previous activity. They may also want to look at the standards for the grades before and after their particular grade. Using the chart below, fill in the necessary information. You may want to look at the online resource "IEP and Lesson Plan Development Handbook of Specially Designed Instruction and Supplementary Aids and Services." http://www.grrec.ky.gov/CaveWeb/pdf_forms/SDI%20SAS.pdf

Unwrapping the CCS Standards

Skills	Concepts	Criteria for Successful Performance	Specially Designed Instruction

What are the tools that we will use?

These are tools that create access and/or provide more intensive supports that ultimately lead to student success and independence. We will be discussing each one in further detail.

- Universal Design for Learning

- Differentiation of Instruction

- Collaborative Practices

- Accommodations

- Assistive Technology

- Specially Designed Instruction Plans

- IEP Matrices

Not Every Child Can Learn!
...by me standing at the front talking
...by working alone
...by reading the textbook
...by worksheets
...by passively taking notes
-D. MARTIN 2013

The Blueprint: Building Powerful IEPs to Increase Student Achievement

CAST UDL at a glance

Transforming education through Universal Design for Learning

www.cast.org

Video Activity

Directions: View the video Universal Design for Learning (UDL) at a glance - http://www.youtube.com/watch?v=bDvKnY0g6e4

The video gives a brief overview of Universal Design for Learning. It will review the basic principles of UDL. UDL is a tool that benefits all students and is based on the curriculum.

UDL at a Glance Video Graphic Organizer

Directions: Fill out the graphic organizer while watching the video.

1. Write down one word from the video that is powerful to you.

2. Write down one sentence that struck a chord with you from the video.

3. Sketch a memorable image from the video below.

Universal Design for Learning

This is a set of principles for curriculum development that give all individuals equal opportunities to learn. UDL is based on brain science that identifies three networks that determine how, what and why we learn.

- Recognition Network – The "what"

- Strategic – "how"

- Affective – "why"

Universal Design for Learning (UDL) is a <u>framework</u> for designing curricula that enable all individuals to gain knowledge, skills, and enthusiasm for learning. UDL provides rich supports for learning and reduces barriers to the curriculum while maintaining high achievement standards for all students." Definition from http://www.cast.org/udl/faq/index.html

Universal Design for Learning

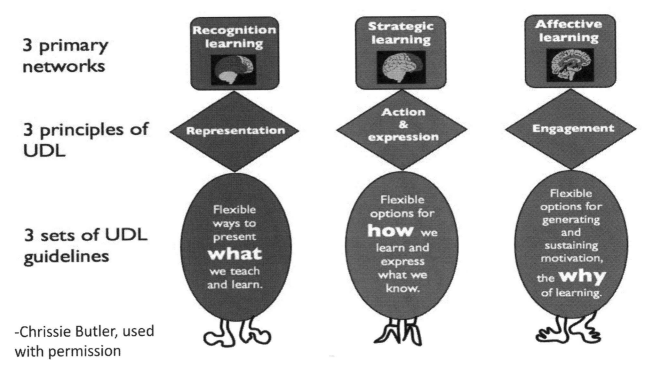

3 primary networks

3 principles of UDL

3 sets of UDL guidelines

-Chrissie Butler, used with permission

This infographic was created by Chrissie Butler and outlines the networks, principles and guidelines of Universal Design for Learning.

UDL – Representation

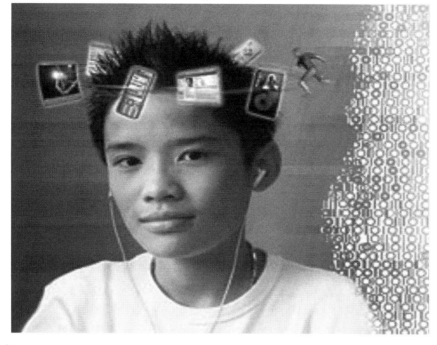

From www.cast.org – "Learners differ in the ways that they perceive and comprehend information that is presented to them."

Principle 1: Multiple Means of Representation – one way of presenting information is not sufficient because all students do not take in information the same way or at the same rate.

Teachers need to consider:

- Perception

- Language, expression, symbols

- Comprehension

UDL – Expression

From www.cast.org – "Learners differ in the ways that they can navigate a learning environment and express what they know."

Principle 2: Multiple Means of Expression – Teachers should recognize that students require strategies, practice and organization in order to act on and express what they know in the classroom.

- Physical action

- Expression and communication

- Executive function

UDL – Engagement

From www.cast.org "…learners differ markedly in the ways in which they can be engaged or motivated to learn."

Principle 3: Multiple Means of Engagement – Some students are stimulated by novelty and spontaneity, while other students benefit from predictable routines.

Teachers need to consider multiple ways to:

- recruit interest

- sustain effort and persistence

- promote self-regulation

UDL "What's In It for Me?

UDL can…

- reduce time needed for making modifications and accommodations

- provide flexible instructional materials, techniques and strategies

- increase student engagement

- address the diversity of learners at the point of curriculum development

- "What's in it for Me" outlines the benefits for the student AND teacher

The Blueprint: Building Powerful IEPs to Increase Student Achievement

Activity: UDL Center Exploration

Directions: Watch the video on learner variability to answer the questions below. Follow the QR code or link and complete the activities. Be able to able to answer the questions below.

http://udlseries.udlcenter.org/presentations/learner_variability.html

Activity 1:

1. Why are curricula limited if they are designed for the 'average' learner?

2. What makes learner variability systematic?

3. Why is it important for educators to know about systematic learner variability?

Activity 2:

http://cast.org/learningtools/index.html

1. Review the tools on this page. Select and sign up for one of the tools on this page.

2. Summarize the tool and explain why you chose to sign up for access to this tool.

3. What other tools on this page will be helpful to you in your professional practice?

UDL – Synthesis/Reflection

Directions: Use the UDL 3 T Chart and the UDL Guidelines to identify the opportunities you have learned about to offer multiple means of representation, expression and engagement.

- How can you offer similar opportunities in your students?

Universal Design for Learning Synthesis/Reflection Horsemanship – Examples of UDL Principles in Action

Multiple Means of Representation	Multiple Means of Expression	Multiple Means of Engagement
Books	Poems	Trail riding
Videos	Journals	Dressage
Clinics	Competitions	Western
Lessons	Videotaping tests and lessons	Hunter/Jumper
Lectures	Scrapbooks	Carriage driving
Apps		Veterinary care
Demonstrations		

Now that you have viewed one of the training videos on the UDL Center website and explored one of the tools, generate a list of the UDL principles in action in this workshop.

Universal Design for Learning Guidelines

Multiple Means of Representation	Multiple Means of Expression	Multiple Means of Engagement

Universal Design for Learning Guidelines

I. Provide Means of Representation	II. Provide Multiple Means of Action and Expression	III. Provide Multiple Means of Engagement
1: Provide options for perception 1.1 Offer ways of customizing the display of information 1.2 Offer alternatives for auditory information 1.3 Offer alternatives for visual information	**4: Provide options for physical action** 4.1 Vary the methods for response and navigation 4.2 Optimize access to tools and assistive technologies	**7: Provide options for recruiting interest** 7.1 Optimize individual choice and autonomy 7.2 Optimize relevance, value, and authenticity 7.3 Minimize threats and distractions
2: Provide options for language, mathematical expressions, and symbols 2.1 Clarify vocabulary and symbols 2.2 Clarify syntax and structure 2.3 Support decoding of text, mathematical notation, and symbols 2.4 Promote understanding across languages 2.5 Illustrate through multiple media	**5: Provide options for expression and communication** 5.1 Use multiple media for communication 5.2 Use multiple tools for construction and composition 5.3 Build fluencies with graduated levels of support for practice and performance	**8: Provide options for sustaining effort and persistence** 8.1 Heighten salience of goals and objectives 8.2 Vary demands and resources to optimize challenge 8.3 Foster collaboration and community 8.4 Increase master-oriented feedback
3: Provide options for comprehension 3.1 Activate or supply background knowledge 3.2 Highlight patterns, critical features, big ideas, and relationships 3.3 Guide information processing, visualization, and manipulation 3.4 Maximize transfer and generalization	**6: Provide options for executive functions** 6.1 Guide appropriate goal-setting 6.2 Support planning and strategy development 6.3 Facilitate managing information and resources 6.4 Enhance capacity for monitoring progress	**9: Provide options for self-regulation** 9.1 Promote expectations and beliefs that optimize motivation 9.2 Facilitate personal coping skills and strategies 9.3 Develop self-assessment and reflection
Resourceful, knowledgeable learners	**Strategic, goal-directed learners**	**Purposeful, motivated learners**

Reflection

- Refer to the previous page with the example of the UDL principles in action. Can you identify the guidelines exemplified under each of the principles?

The Blueprint: Building Powerful IEPs to Increase Student Achievement
All Rights Reserved/ www.crec.org

Differentiation

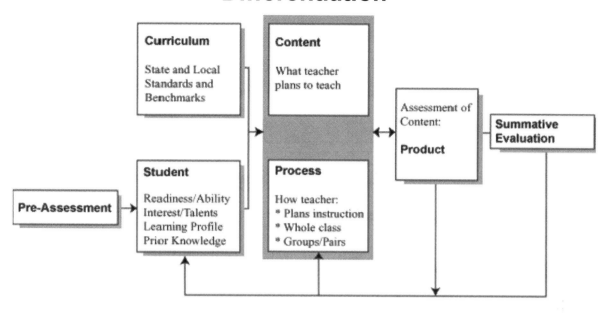

Source: Differentiated Instruction and Implications for UDL Implementation
By Tracey Hall, Nicole Strangman, and Anne Meyer, *1/14/11*

Reflection

- What do you notice about the process and flow of differentiated instruction?

Please view the video of Rick Wormelli summarizing some important aspects of differentiation (http://youtu.be/huFrNwRfpxc). You should listen to the video and check off the characteristics of the differentiated classroom as you view it in the video.

pre-assess	application of learning	set a goal for learning
clear expectations	student ownership	model
context	share big ideas	connections to real life
high standards for all	formative assessment	visual, auditory, kinesthetic
tiering	scaffolding	engagement
meaningful	relevant	varied complexity of tasks
multiple pathways to the same high standards		

UDL vs. Differentiation

UDL begins with the curriculum

DI begins with the student

Review the graphic on Similarities and Differences between UDL and Differentiation. Do you perceive an advantage of one method over the other?

Similarities

☐ meet individual needs

☐ equal access to high quality content and instruction

☐ highly supported engaging learning environments

☐ multiple ways to express knowledge and skills

☐ emphasize critical thinking and strategic learning

☐ assess student progress during learning

Differences

☐ UDL addresses learner diversity at the point of curriculum

☐ UDL builds differentiation into the curriculum

☐ UDL provides learners with tools to take charge of their learning

"Nesting Laws" Accommodations

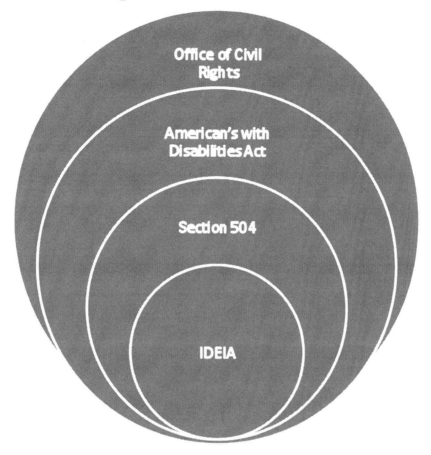

This graphic organizer depicts how the laws that govern entitlement to reasonable accommodations are interrelated. For example, IDEIA is a subset of section 504. Therefore, children protected by IDEIA are also protected by Section 504. IDEIA is more specific. If a child needs accommodations, that falls into section 504 and IDEIA. A child might also receive modifications that may not apply to Section 504.

Modifications and Accommodations

It is not unusual for the terms "modification" and "accommodation" to be used inter-changeably. It is very important to make a clear distinction between the two.

Modification – "changes the target skill or the construct of interest. Modifications often reduce learning expectations or affect the content in such a way that what is being taught or tested is fundamentally changed." (Crawford, L. NCLD)

Accommodation – "allows the student to demonstrate what he or she knows without fundamentally changing the target skill that's being taught in the classroom or measured in testing situations. Accommodations do not reduce learning or performance expectations that we might hold for students." (Crawford, L. NCLD)

Instructional Accommodations

An instructional accommodation is a practice or procedure that allows a student with a disability to have equitable access to instruction and assessment. An accommodation is "intended to reduce or eliminate the effects of the student's disability." Accommodations do not reduce learner expectations. (Thompson, Morse, Sharpe & Hall 2005)

    Step 1 – Expect students to achieve

    Step 2 – What are accommodations?

    Step 3 - Select

    Step 4 – Administer

    Step 5 – Evaluate

Step 1 – Accommodations

- Expect all students with disabilities to achieve.

- Appropriate accommodations help students access grade level content.

Step 2 – What are Accommodations?

- Types of accommodations:

  - ✓ Presentation – Allow students to access information in ways that do not require them to visually read standard print.

  - ✓ Response – Allow students to use assistive devices or organizers to complete activities, assignments and assessments.

  - ✓ Setting – Change the location or conditions of an assessment setting.

✓ Timing and Scheduling – Increase the length of allowable time to complete an assignment or assessment. This may also involve changing the way the time is organized. (Thompson, Morse, Sharpe & Hall 2005 p. 14)

Resources:

- Section 504 accommodation information: www2.ed.gov/about/offices/list/ocr/504faq.html

- See IDEIA accommodation information: www.osepideasthatwork.org/parentkit/school_accom_mods_eng.asp

- See Section 504 accommodation information:

Step 3 – Select Accommodations

- What works?

- What will the student accept?

- What is acceptable for high stakes tests?

Resources: There is also a reference to help educators with Do's and Don'ts of selecting appropriate accommodations. A pdf of the manual can be found by following this link: http://www.ccsso.org/Documents/2005/Accommodations_Manual_How_2005.pdf

Don Johnston's website provides a free download of a manual that will help you to determine appropriate accommodations for students with disabilities in the area of reading. This website will take you to the free download: http://www.donjohnston.com/products/par/index.html

Steps 4 and 5

- Administer and evaluate the effectiveness of the accommodations

Collaborative Practices

- Consultation

- Co-Planning

- Co-Teaching

Activity

Directions: List all the things we do that require collaboration all start with "co". Brainstorm 25 "co" words.

1.

2.

3.

4.

5.

6.

7.

8.

9.

10.

11.

12.

13.

14.

15.

16.

17.

18.

19.

20.

21.

22.

23.

24.

25.

1. Circle your top five and use them in one sentence.

2. **Write your sentence below.** Example: Communication will prevent conflict and this will allow you to constantly, and cooperatively collaborate with your co-teacher.

Assistive Technology

"...any item, piece of equipment, or product system, whether acquired commercially off the shelf, modified, or customized, that is used to increase, maintain, or improve functional capabilities of a child with disabilities."

Decision Making Process

WATI Planning Guide   # SETT Framework

Activity

View each of these tools by reading each one of the QR codes using a QR code reader and a smart phone or tablet or by going to the following websites:

- **WATI Planning Guide** - http://assistivetech-4alllearners.wikispaces.com/file/view/WATI-Plguide.pdf/78801567/WATI-Plguide.pdf

- **SETT Framework** - http://assistivetech-4alllearners.wikispaces.com/file/view/SETT%20framework.pdf/78801849/SETT%20framework.pdf

After looking at the tools answer the following questions:

1. What do they have in common?

2. Do participants have a preference?

3. What process do school systems currently use to make determinations about appropriate assistive technology for students?

Special Education

"….Defined, as a term of art, in the IDEIA regulations at 34 CFR 300.39(a) *as **specially designed instruction**, at no cost to the parents, to meet the unique needs of a child with a disability,* including (a) instruction conducted in the classroom, in the home, in hospitals and institutions, and in other settings; and (b) instruction in **physical education**…..CFR 300.39(a)(2)(i)-(iii). …"

Specially Designed Instruction

"Included in the definition of **special education** in Part B regulations at 34 CFR 300.39(b)(3) as **adapting**, as appropriate to the needs of an eligible **child** under Part B of the IDIEA, the *content, methodology, or delivery of instruction to address the unique needs of the child that result from the child's disability and to ensure access of the child to the general curriculum*…"

Remember that special education is specially designed instruction!

When more intensive support is needed

- Specially Designed Instruction Plans

- IEP Matrices

Specially Designed Instruction Plans

Access to instruction related to the standards will increase if educational teams use the tools and methods discussed in this workbook. However, many students with disabilities will still require some type of specially designed instruction. This is necessitated by the unique needs of the child's disability. Just like the other methods and tools that have been discussed so far, specially designed needs to be preplanned and created through collaboration with other professionals on the child's educational team.

IEP Matrix: Embedding Specially Designed Instruction

The purpose of the specially designed instruction plan is to create an explicit format for planning, embedding and monitoring the implementation of specially designed instruction needed for a student's IEP goals and objectives.

Difference between embedded instruction and teachable moments

Embedded Instruction

Teachable Moments

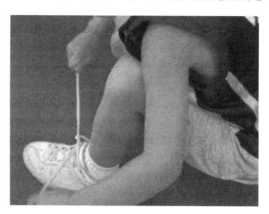

Developing an IEP Matrix

Look at the child's goals and/or objectives and determine:

- During what activities will we be able to provide instruction

- Who, where and when to collect data on these objectives

  - Educators write in a student's daily schedule and the target objectives that the team is focusing on at that time. This is a fluid document meant to facilitate embedding instruction into the appropriate activities during the school day and data collection. Individual children will have different numbers of target behaviors that are currently identified for the focus of instruction. Simply make the matrix larger or smaller as needed to address the individual child's plan.

Activity

Use the blank handout to brainstorm about one goal or objective from a student's IEP and how it can be embedded throughout the school day given that student's schedule. For example, the student may need to learn to initiate a greeting with a peer or adult. When are there naturally occurring opportunities during the school day where an instructional plan can be put in to place and data can be collected?

Individual Child Activity Matrix

Child's Name: _____ Date: _____

Teacher or Classroom: _____

	Target Behavior 1	Target Behavior 2	Target Behavior 3	Target Behavior 4	Target Behavior 5
Schedule					

Exit Activity: Choose One

Create an Instagram video to summarize your learning from Module 3. Instagram is a social networking app that allows users to post photos and 15 second videos to a feed that followers can view and comment on. Set up an Instagram account using a valid email address and a password.

Create and IEP Matrix or a Specially Designed Instruction Plan for a student that you instruct.

Education is not preparation for life;
education is life itself.
-JOHN DEWEY

Reflections to Inform Your Practice

1. Summarize the important aspects of creating instruction from the CCS.

2. What practices am I going to apply in my job or what experiences will I try?

3. What did I try and did it work why or why not?

4. What will I try next?

Assess Your Learning

Module 3 – Creating Instruction from the Common Core Standards for Special Education and Related Services

1. What is the difference between a modification and an accommodation?

2. What grade level standards should I use as a reference for a student who is functioning significantly below their actual grade level?

Answers to Assess Your Learning

Module 3 – Creating Instruction from the Common Core Standards for Special Education and Related Services

1. **What is the difference between a modification and an accommodation?**

   This is a question that can be addressed in all four modules. Teachers, administrators and related service personnel frequently interchange these two terms and it is important to clarify the language being used as it has a significant impact on student services and supports. An accommodation is "a change that helps a student overcome or work around the disability." (NICHCY 2013). A modification is a "a change in what is being taught or expected from the student." (NICHCY 2013)

2. **What grade level standards should I use as a reference for a student who is functioning significantly below their actual grade level?**

   This is also a question that may come up in Module 2. It is important for teachers to know the expectations for the grade level standards that corresponds to the grade level in which the child in enrolled. However, it is possible for the educational team to look back at standards for earlier grades to compare the progression of skills for that standard in relation to the student's current performance. Also, many states are producing documents that help teams determine appropriate entry points into the standards for students with significant disabilities. You can refer to documents produced by the Massachusetts Department of Education (http://www.doe.mass.edu/mcas/alt/resources.html). Also, Utah has published this reference document (http://www.schools.utah.gov/sars/DOCS/resources/ext-corestd.aspx).

   The bottom line is that educational teams must consider the appropriate grade level standards when designing an individualized program for a student with significant disabilities that allows that student to participate in grade level instruction to the extent appropriate.

Building Powerful IEPs to Increase Student Achievement

Module 4
Collecting Data and Monitoring of the IEP Progress

In this Module you will

- ✓ Identify ways to collect data to monitor student progress

- ✓ Understand how progress monitoring is connected to data collection and accountability of the IEP

- ✓ Define the seven steps to progress monitoring the IEP

- ✓ Analyze your IEPs to determine if they meet the data collection criteria

- ✓ List, rank and categorize the important assessments that you administer to students during the year

- ✓ Learn measurement types and tools and where to locate them

- ✓ Complete a data collection schedule and data collection worksheet

Module 4 Collecting Data and Monitoring of the IEP Progress

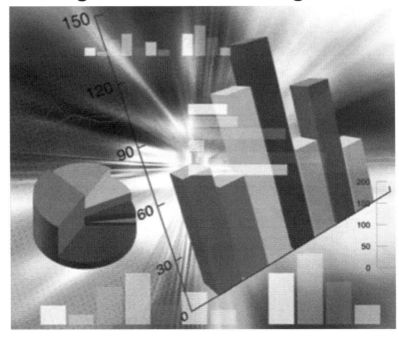

"It is a capital mistake to theorize before one has data."

-ARTHUR CONAN DOYLE, SR., SCOTTISH WRITER
AND CREATOR OF THE SHERLOCK HOLMES 1859-1930

This quote was selected to emphasize the importance of using data to inform instructional decisions about student programs.

Questions I Hope Get Answered

What are the questions or concerns you have about data collection and monitoring of the IEP that you hope will be addressed?

Progress Monitoring: Assessment, Data Collection and Informing Instruction and Practice

- Progress monitoring remains a required part of the IEP with IDEIA 2004

- Other provisions in IDEIA 2004 mandate greater accountability for student progress

  - Results-oriented shift

  - Outcomes

IDEIA 2004 states the IEP must include a statement of how the child's progress toward the annual goals will be measured (20 U.S.C.§ 1414(d)(1)(A)). The IEP must also state how progress will be reported to the family and to what extent will that progress be considered to be sufficient (20U.S.C. § 1414(d)(1)(A)(i)(III)).

In regards to legal decisions about progress monitoring, courts have been unwilling to accept school district assertions concerning the appropriateness of a student's program absent proof in the form of data (Zelin, 2000).

Activity Venn Diagram

The purpose of this activity is to help you to consider the process of progress monitoring and how it is connected to the data collection and accountability in the IEP.

Directions: Read the articles, *Progress Monitoring: Legal Issues and Recommendations for IEP Teams* and *What is Scientifically Research-Based Research on Progress Monitoring?* provided and write details that tell how the articles are different in the outer circles. Write details that tell how the articles are alike where the circles overlap.

Venn Diagram

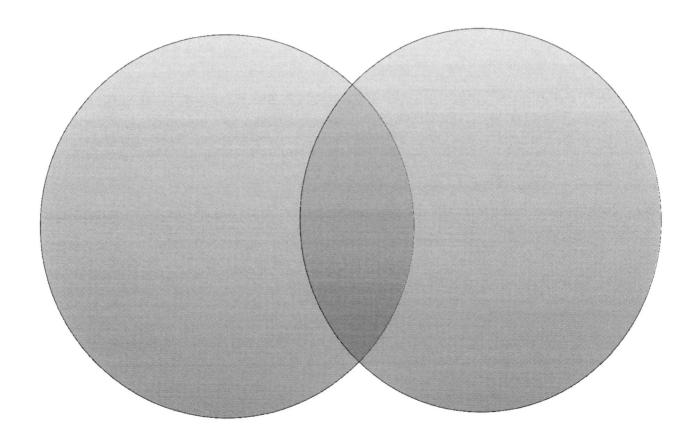

National Center on Student Progress Monitoring

What Is Scientifically-Based Research on Progress Monitoring?
Lynn S. Fuchs and Douglas Fuchs

Abstract. When teachers use systematic progress monitoring to track their students progress in reading, mathematics, or spelling, they are better able to identify students in need of additional or different forms of instruction, they design stronger instructional programs, and their students achieve better. This document first describes progress monitoring procedures for which experimental evidence demonstrates these effects. Then, an overview of the research is presented.

Introduction. Progress monitoring is when teachers assess students' academic performance on a regular basis (weekly or monthly) for two purposes: to determine whether children are profiting appropriately from the typical instructional program and to build more effective programs for the children who benefit inadequately from typical instruction.

This document describes research on progress monitoring in the areas of reading, spelling, and mathematics at grades 1-6. Experimental research, which documents how teachers can use progress monitoring to enhance student progress, is available for one form of progress monitoring: Curriculum-Based Measurement (CBM). More than 200 empirical studies published in peer-review journals (a) provide evidence of CBM's reliability and validity for assessing the development of competence in reading, spelling, and mathematics and (b) document

CBM's capacity to help teachers improve student outcomes at the elementary grades.

Most classroom assessment relies on mastery measurement. With mastery measurement, teachers test for mastery of a single skill and, after mastery is demonstrated, they assess mastery of the next skill in a sequence. So, at different times of the school year, different skills are assessed. Because the nature and difficulty of the tests keep changing with successive mastery, test scores from different times of the school cannot be compared (e.g., scores earned in September cannot be compared to scores earned in November or February or May). This makes it impossible to quantify or describe rates of progress. Furthermore, mastery measurement has unknown reliability and validity, and it fails to provide information about whether students are maintaining the previously mastered skills.

CBM avoids these problems because, instead of measuring mastery of a series of single short-term objectives, each CBM test assesses all the different skills covered in the annual curriculum. CBM samples the many skills in the annual curriculum in such a way that each weekly test is an alternate form (with different test items, but of equivalent difficulty). So, in September, a CBM mathematics test assesses all of the computation, money, graphs/charts, and problem-solving skills to be covered during the entire year. In November or February or May, the CBM test samples the annual

Providing information and technical assistance to implement progress monitoring for students in the elementary grades.
1000 Thomas Jefferson ~ Washington, DC 20007
202-342-5000
E-Mail: studentprogress@air.org Web: www.studentprogress.org

curriculum in exactly the same way (but with different items). Therefore, scores earned at different times during the school year can be compared to determine whether a student's competence is increasing.

CBM also differs from mastery measurement because it is standardized; that is, the progress monitoring procedures for creating tests, for administering and scoring those tests, and for summarizing and interpreting the resulting database are prescribed. By relying on standardized methods and by sampling the annual curriculum on every test, CBM produces a broad range of scores across individuals of the same age. The rank ordering of students on CBM corresponds with rank orderings on other important criteria of student competence (1). For example, students who score high (or low) on CBM are the same students who score high (or low) on the annual state tests. For these reasons, CBM demonstrates strong reliability and validity (2). At the same time, because each CBM test assesses the many skills embedded in the annual curriculum, CBM yields descriptions of students' strengths and weaknesses on each of the many skills contained in the curriculum. These skills profiles also demonstrate reliability and validity (3). The measurement tasks within CBM are as follows:

Pre-reading

Phoneme segmentation fluency: For 1 minute, the examiner says words; in response to each word, the child says the sounds that constitute the word.

Letter sound fluency: The examiner presents the student with a sheet of paper showing the 26 lower case letters displayed in random order; the student has 1 minute to say the sound identified with each letter.

Reading

Word identification fluency: The examiner presents the student with a list of words, randomly sampled (with replacement) from a list of high-frequency words; the student reads words aloud for 1 minute; the score is the number of words read correctly. (Word identification fluency is appropriate for first graders until the score reaches 40 words read correctly per minute.)

Passage reading fluency: The examiner presents the student with a passage of the difficulty expected for year-end competence; the student reads aloud for 1 minute; the score is the number of words read correctly. (Passage reading fluency is appropriate through the fourth-grade instructional level.)

Maze fluency: The examiner presents the student with a passage of the difficulty expected for year-end competence for 2.5 minutes; from this passage, every seventh word has been deleted and replaced with three possible choices; the student reads the passage while selecting the meaningful choice for every seventh word; the score is the number of correct replacements.

Mathematics

Computation: The examiner presents the student with items systematically sampling the problems covered in the annual curriculum (adding, subtracting, multiplying, dividing whole numbers, fractions, and decimals, depending on grade); the student has a fixed time (depending on grade) to write answers; the score is the number of correct digits written in answers.

Concepts and applications: The examiner presents the student with items systematically sampling the problems covered in the annual curriculum (measurement, money, charts/graphs, problem solving, numeration, number concepts); the student has a fixed time (depending on grade) to write answers; the score is the number of correct answers written.

Spelling

Each test comprises 20 words randomly sampled from the pool of words expected for mastery during the year; the examiner dictates a word while the student spells on paper; the next item is presented after the student completes his/her spelling or after 10

The Blueprint: Building Powerful IEPs to Increase Student Achievement

seconds, whichever occurs sooner; the test lasts 2 minutes; the score is the number of correct letter sequences (pairs of letters) spelled correctly.

Written Expression

In response to a story starter (i.e., a short topic sentence or phrase to begin the written piece), the student writes for a fixed amount of time (3–10 minutes). The score is the number of correct word sequences.

CBM produces two kinds of information. The overall CBM score (i.e., total score on the test) is an overall indicator of competence. The CBM skills profile describes strengths and weaknesses on the various skills assessed on each CBM test.

Teachers use the **overall CBM score** in three ways.

First, overall CBM scores are used in universal screening to identify students in need of additional or different forms of instruction. For example, CBM can be administered to all students in a class, school, or district at one point in time (e.g., October or January). Then, children in need of additional attention are identified using (a) normative standards (i.e., identifying students who score low compared to other students in the class, school, or nation) or (b) CBM benchmarks (i.e., identifying students whose scores fall below a specific cut-point that predicts future success on state tests).

The second way teachers use overall CBM scores is to monitor students' development of academic competence. That is, students are measured weekly or monthly, with each student's CBM scores graphed against time. This graph shows the student's progress toward achieving competence on the annual curriculum. If the graphed scores are going up, then the student is developing competence on the annual curriculum; if the scores are flat, then the student is failing to benefit from the instructional program. The

rate of weekly improvement is quantified as slope. Research provides estimates of the amount of CBM progress (or slope) students typically make. So, a teacher can compare the slope of her/his own class to the slope of large numbers of typically developing students to determine whether his/her instructional program is generally successful or requires adjustment. Teachers can also examine the slopes of individual students to determine which children are failing to make the amount of progress other children in the class (or nation) are demonstrating and therefore require additional help.

The third way teachers use overall CBM scores is to improve instructional programs. For students who are failing to profit from the standard instructional program (as demonstrated via universal CBM screening or via inadequate CBM progress-monitoring slopes), teachers use CBM to "experiment" with different instructional components. As teachers adjust instructional programs, in an attempt to enhance academic progress for these children, the teachers continue to collect CBM data. They then compare CBM slopes for different instructional components to identify which components optimize academic growth. In this way, teachers use CBM to build effective programs for otherwise difficult-to-teach children.

Teachers use the **CBM skills profiles** to identify which skills in the annual curriculum require additional instruction and which students are experiencing problems with maintaining skills after initial mastery was demonstrated. This kind of information can be accessed via CBM because every test assesses every skill covered in the annual curriculum. So, mastery status on every skill can be described directly from each CBM test.

Overview of research. Studies included in this overview met the following criteria. First, they relied on experimental design; that is, teachers volunteered to participate in any of the study conditions and then were randomly assigned to conditions. Second, all studies included a control group (where teachers did not use systematic progress monitoring), against which the effects of progress monitoring procedures were assessed. Third, progress monitoring procedures were implemented for at least 15 school weeks, or 4 school months. Fourth, teachers' instructional plans were analyzed to determine how planning changed as a function of progress monitoring. Fifth, students' academic achievement was measured at the beginning and end of the study on global tests to determine whether students achieved differently in the various progress monitoring conditions.

This overview is organized in three sections: (a) evidence on CBM's utility to identify students in need of additional or different forms of instruction, (b) evidence on the usefulness of CBM's graphed analysis of the overall score to help teachers improve their instructional programs and effect better student achievement, and (c) evidence on the added value of CBM's skills profiles for designing superior instructional programs that produce greater learning.

Results of these studies are described in terms of statistical significance and effect sizes. Statistical significance means that one treatment group performed so much better than another group that it is highly unlikely that the results could be attributed to chance. This speaks to the reliability of the findings: If a similar study were conducted again, we would expect to find similar results, and if a teacher were to implement the treatment, we would expect similar effects for her/his students. It is possible, however, to have a statistically significant effect, which is accurate and reliable, but is small.

To address the question about whether a treatment effect is big or small, we look at effect sizes. Effect sizes tell us how many standard deviations one treatment group

performed better than another. If the mean of a test is 100 and its standard deviation is 15 (like an IQ test), then an effect size of 1 standard deviation would mean, for example, that the treatment group ended the study with a score of 100 while the control group ended with a score of 85. Generally, in educational research, an effect size of .30 is considered small, .50 is considered moderate, and .70 is considered large.

Identifying students in need of additional or different forms of instruction. Research shows that CBM can be used to prompt teacher concern about student progress and to signal the need for additional or different forms of instruction. For example, in a recent study (4), 24 second-grade teachers were randomly assigned to control or CBM progress monitoring groups. Progress monitoring teachers, with the assistance of computers, collected CBM oral reading fluency data with every student in their classes. The computer organized the CBM information into individual student graphs as well as class reports. These reports showed CBM class graphs; noted students who fell in the lowest quartile of the class; and identified students in need of comprehension instruction, fluency development, or decoding work. In addition, the report provided a rank ordering of the students in the class, sorting them into those who already had met the year-end CBM benchmark, those who were on track to meet the year-end benchmark, and those who were at risk of failing to achieve the year-end benchmark. Teachers collected CBM data for 15 weeks, with individual graphs shown at the end of every data-collection session and with class reports printed every 3 weeks. Every 3 weeks, teachers answered the questions, "Do you have children whose progress seems problematic? Which children are you concerned about?" Progress monitoring teachers expressed concern about statistically significantly more students, with effect sizes exceeding 1 standard deviation. Moreover, when asked, "Why are you concerned about _____ ?," Progress monitoring teachers described features of student performance to explain their concern; by contrast, control teachers cited reasons beyond their control (such as English Language Learner status, special education status, attention or motivation problems, or inadequate parental involvement). This pattern of results was statistically significant. Therefore, systematic progress monitoring can be used to raise teacher concern about students' reading progress and to signal the need for additional or different forms of instruction.

Usefulness of graphed analysis of thee overall CBM scores. Evidence strongly supports the utility of graphed analysis of overall CBM scores in helping teachers plan more effective programs. Studies (5) conducted over the past decade provide corroborating evidence of strong effects on students' reading, spelling, and mathematics achievement when teachers rely on CBM progress monitoring to help them plan their instruction. A study conducted in the New York City Public Schools (6) illustrates this research. Teachers participated for 18 weeks in a control group (i.e., no systematic progress monitoring) or a CBM progress monitoring group. In the progress monitoring group, teachers measured students' reading performance with CBM oral reading fluency twice weekly, scored and graphed CBM performances, and applied CBM decision rules (described in the next three paragraphs) to those graphs to plan their students' reading programs. Children whose teachers employed CBM progress monitoring to develop reading programs achieved statistically significantly better than students in the control group on measures tapping a variety of reading skills, including a fluency test as well as the decoding and comprehension subtests of the Stanford Diagnostic Reading Test. Effect sizes were large, ranging between .94 and 1.18 standard deviations. So, teachers used CBM's graphed analysis to effect greater reading achievement in terms of fluency, decoding, and comprehension.

CBM progress monitoring, using the graphed analysis, relies on decision rules that help teachers set ambitious student goals and help them determine when instructional adjustments are needed to prompt better student growth. The student's initial CBM scores are graphed. The teacher uses normative information about expected rates of CBM growth to set a goal for the end of the school year. A diagonal line is drawn from the initial scores to the goal level/date. This diagonal line represents the desired rate of improvement for that student. As the instructional program is implemented, weekly CBM data are collected and graphed. A line of best fit is drawn through the student's graphed scores to estimate the child's actual weekly rate of improvement, or CBM slope. The steepness of the goal line is compared to the steepness of the student's actual rate of improvement. If the steepness of the student's actual rate of improvement is greater, then the CBM decision is to raise the goal. If the steepness of the goal line is greater, then the CBM decision is to adjust the instructional program to stimulate greater learning.

Fuchs, Fuchs, and Hamlett (7) explored the contribution of the goal-raising CBM decision rule. Teachers were assigned randomly to and participated in one of three treatments for 15 weeks in mathematics: no CBM, CBM without a goal-raising rule, and CBM with a goal-raising rule. The goal-raising rule required teachers to increase goals whenever the student's actual rate of growth (represented by the slope through the actual, graphed scores) was greater than the growth rate anticipated by the teacher (reflected in the goal line). Teachers in the CBM goal-raising condition raised goals statistically significantly more frequently (for 15 of 30 students) than teachers in the nongoal-raising conditions (for 1 of 30 students). Moreover, concurrent with teachers' goal raising was statistically significantly differential student achievement on pre/post standardized achievement tests: The effect size comparing the pre/post change of the two CBM conditions (i.e., with and without the goal-raising rule) was .50 standard deviation. Consequently, using CBM to monitor the appropriateness of instructional goals and to adjust goals upward whenever possible is one means by which CBM can be used to assist teachers in their instructional planning.

A second way in which CBM can be used to enhance instructional decisions is to assess the adequacy of student progress and determine whether, and if so when, instructional adjustments are necessary. When actual growth rate is less than expected growth rate, the teacher modifies the instructional program to promote stronger learning. Fuchs, Fuchs, and Hamlett (8) estimated the contribution of this CBM decision-making strategy with 29 teachers who implemented CBM for 15 school weeks with 53 students. Teachers in a "CBM-measurement only" group measured students' reading growth as required but did not use the assessment information to structure students' reading programs. Teachers in the CBM-"change the program" group measured student performance and used CBM to determine when to introduce program adjustments to enhance student learning. Results indicated that, although teachers in both groups monitored student progress, important differences were associated with the use of the "change the program" decision rule. As shown on the Stanford Achievement Test-Reading Comprehension subtest, students in the "change the program" group achieved statistically significantly better than a no-CBM control group (effect size=.72), whereas the "measurement only" CBM group did not (effect size=.36). Moreover, the slopes of the two CBM treatment groups were significantly different, favoring the achievement of the "change the program" group (effect size=.86). As suggested by

these findings and results of other studies (9), collecting CBM data, in and of itself, exerts only a small effect on student learning. To enhance student outcomes in substantial ways, teachers need to use the CBM data to build effective programs for difficult-to-teach students.

Added value of skills profiles. To obtain rich descriptions of student performance, alternative ways of summarizing and describing student performance are necessary. Because CBM assesses performance on the year's curriculum at each testing, rich descriptions of strengths and weaknesses in the curriculum can be generated, and studies show how these skills profiles enhance teacher planning and student learning. In a series of investigations in reading (10), math (11), and spelling (12), teachers were assigned randomly to one of three conditions: no CBM, CBM with goal-raising and change-the-program decision rules, and CBM with goal-raising and change-the-program decision rules plus CBM skills profiles. In all three studies, teachers in the skills profile group generated instructional plans that were statistically significantly more varied and more responsive to individuals' learning needs. Moreover, they effected statistically significantly better student learning as measured on change between pre- and posttest performance on global measures of achievement. Effect sizes associated with the CBM diagnostic profile groups ranged from .65 to 1.23 standard deviations. This series of studies demonstrates how structured, well-organized CBM information about students' strengths and difficulties in the curriculum can help teachers build better programs and effect greater learning.

Summary. As demonstrated via the randomized field trials described above, teachers can use systematic progress monitoring in reading, mathematics, and spelling to identify students in need of additional or different forms of instruction, to design stronger instructional programs, and to effect better achievement outcomes for their students.

References.

1. Good, R.H., Simmons, D.C., & Kame'enui, E.J. (2001). The importance and decision-making utility of a continuum of fluency-based indicators of foundational reading skills for third-grade high-stakes outcomes. *Scientific Studies of Reading, 5,* 257-288.

2. Marston, D. (1989). Curriculum-based measurement: What is it and why do it? In M.R. Shinn (Eds.), *Curriculum-based measurement: Assessing special children* (pp. 18-78). New York: Guilford.

3. Fuchs, L.S., Fuchs, D., Hamlett, C.L., & Allinder, R.M. (1989). The reliability and validity of skills analysis within curriculum-based measurement. *Diagnostique, 14,* 203-221.

   Fuchs, L.S., Fuchs, D., Hamlett, C.L., Thompson, A., Roberts, P.H., Kubec, P., & Stecker, P.M. (1994). Technical features of a mathematics concepts and applications curriculum-based measurement system. *Diagnostique, 19*(4), 23-49.

4. Fuchs, L.S., & Fuchs, D. (in press). Can diagnostic assessment information enhance general educators' instructional planning and student achievement. In B. Foorman (Ed.), *Prevention and intervention for reading disabilities.* New York: York Press.

5. Fuchs, L.S., Fuchs, D., Hamlett, C.L., & Allinder, R.M. (1991). Effects of expert system advice within curriculum-based measurement on teacher planning and student achievement in spelling. *School Psychology Review, 20,* 49-66.

   Fuchs, L.S., Fuchs, D., Hamlett, C.L., & Ferguson, C. (1992). Effects of expert system consultation within curriculum-based measurement using a reading maze task. *Exceptional Children, 58,* 436-450.

   Jones, E.D., & Krouse, J.P. (1988). The effectiveness of data-based instruction by student teachers in classrooms for pupils with mild learning handicaps. *Teacher Education and Special Education, 11,* 9-19.

   Stecker, P.M., & Fuchs, L.S. (2000). Effecting superior achievement using curriculum-based measurement: The importance of individual progress monitoring. *Learning Disability Research and Practice, 15,* 128-134.

   Wesson, C.L. (1991). Curriculum-based measurement and two models of follow-up consultation. *Exceptional Children, 57,* 246-257.

   Wesson, C.L., Skiba, R., Sevcik, B., King, R., & Deno, S. (1984). The effects of technically adequate instructional data on achievement. *Remedial and Special Education, 5,* 17-22.

6. Fuchs, L.S., Deno, S.L., & Mirkin, P.K. (1984). The effects of frequent curriculum-based measurement and evaluation on student achievement, pedagogy, and student awareness of learning. *American Educational Research Journal, 21,* 449-460.

7. Fuchs, L.S., Fuchs, D., & Hamlett, C.L. (1989a). Effects of alternative goal structures within curriculum-based measurement. *Exceptional Children, 55*, 429-438.

8. Fuchs, L.S., Fuchs, D., & Hamlett, C.L. (1989b). Effects of instrumental use of curriculum-based measurement to enhance instructional programs. *Remedial and Special Education, 10*(2), 43-52.

9. Stecker, P.M., & Fuchs, L.S. (2000). Effecting superior achievement using curriculum-based measurement: The importance of individual progress monitoring. *Learning Disability Research and Practice, 15*, 128-134.

   Wesson, C.L., Skiba, R., Sevcik, B., King, R., & Deno, S. (1984). The effects of technically adequate instructional data on achievement. *Remedial and Special Education, 5*, 17-22.

10. Fuchs, L.S., Fuchs, D., & Hamlett, C.L. (1989). Monitoring reading growth using student recalls: Effects of two teacher feedback systems. *Journal of Educational Research*, 83, 103-111.

11. Fuchs, L.S., Fuchs, D., Hamlett, C.L., & Stecker, P.M. (1990). The role of skills analysis in curriculum-based measurement in math. *School Psychology Review, 19*, 6-22.

12. Fuchs, L.S., Fuchs, D., Hamlett, C.L., & Allinder, R.M. (1991). The contribution of skills analysis to curriculum-based measurement in spelling. *Exceptional Children, 57*, 443-452.

Implications for Practice.

- Teachers should monitor student progress in reading, spelling, and mathematics using standardized progress monitoring systems, such as curriculum-based measurement (CBM).

- Teachers should use progress monitoring systems to identify students in need of additional or different forms of instruction.

- For students who do not respond adequately to the standard instructional program, teachers should use graphed analyses of CBM scores to insure ambitious goals and to identify instructional components that result in improved learning for otherwise difficult-to-teach students.

- Teachers should use skills profiles, derived from progress monitoring systems, to formulate strong instructional programs and to effect better student outcomes.

The Blueprint: Building Powerful IEPs to Increase Student Achievement

Additional Readings.

Deno, S.L. (1985). Curriculum-based measurement: The emerging alternative. *Exceptional Children, 52,* 219–232.

Deno, S.L., & Fuchs, L.S. (1987). Developing curriculum-based measurement systems for data-based special education problem solving. *Focus on Exceptional Children, 19*(8), 1–16.

Fuchs, L.S., & Deno, S.L. (1991). Paradigmatic distinctions between instructionally relevant measurement models. *Exceptional Children, 57,* 488–501.

Fuchs, L.S., Fuchs, D., Hamlett, C.L., Walz, L., & Germann, G. (1993). Formative evaluation of academic progress: How much growth can we expect? *School Psychology Review, 22,* 27–48.

Good, R.H., Simmons, D.C., & Kame'enui, E.J. (2001). The importance and decision-making utility of a continuum of fluency-based indicators of foundational reading skills for third-grade high-stakes outcomes. *Scientific Studies of Reading, 5,* 257–288.

This document was developed through Cooperative Agreement (#H324U010004) between Vanderbilt University and the U.S. Department of Education, Office of Special Education Programs for the National Research Center on Learning Disabilities. The contents of this document do not necessarily reflect the views or policies of the Department of Education, nor does mention of trade names, commercial products, or organizations imply endorsement by the U.S. Government.

U.S. Office of Special Education Programs

What is Scientifically-Based Research on Progress Monitoring?

9

Progress Monitoring: Legal Issues and Recommendations for IEP Teams

Progress Monitoring: Legal Issues and Recommendations for IEP Teams

Susan K. Etscheidt

TEACHING Exceptional Children, Vol. 38, No. 3, pp. 56-60. Copyright 2006 CEC.

Progress monitoring is essential to evaluating the appropriateness of a child's individualized education program (IEP), yet many IEP teams fail to develop or implement progress monitoring plans, improperly delegate such responsibilities, or use inappropriate measurements to determine student progress. Not all IEP teams plan or implement progress monitoring for behavior intervention plans. Those teams that do include progress monitoring often do not meet federal requirements, or their practices do not provide meaningful data. How can we improve IEP progress monitoring for students with disabilities?

Both the Individuals With Disabilities Education Act of 1997 (IDEA) and the 2004 Individuals With Disabilities Education Improvement Act (IDEIA) require that a student's individualized education program (IEP) include:

- A statement of the child's present level of academic achievement and functional performance;
- A statement of measurable annual goals;
- A statement of the special education, related and supplemental services to be provided to the child;

- An explanation of the extent, if any, to which the child will not participate with nondisabled children in the regular class and in the activities;
- A statement of any individual appropriate accommodations that are necessary to measure the academic achievement and functional performance of the child on state and district-wide assessments;
- A statement of dates and duration of services provided;
- Appropriate, measurable post-secondary goals and the transition services to be provided; and
- A statement of how the child's progress toward the annual goals will be measured (20 U.S.C. § 1414(d)(1)(A)).

The progress monitoring provision also requires that the IEP specify how the child's parents will be regularly informed of the child's progress toward the goals, and the extent to which progress is considered sufficient (20 U.S.C. § 1414(d)(1)(A)(i)(III)). Progress monitoring helps IEP teams address any lack of expected progress toward the annual goals of the Code of Federal Regulations (1999) (34 C.F.R. § 300.324(b)(1)) and make decisions concerning the effectiveness of curriculum delivery (Peck & Scarpati, 2005).

Progress monitoring is essential to evaluating the appropriateness of a child's program, yet there is less compliance with this required component of the IEP than any other (Yell, 1998), and current progress monitoring practices often fail to produce vital and meaningful data (Pemberton, 2003).

Legal Decisions

Several administrative and judicial decisions have focused on the absence of adequate progress monitoring. In general, courts have been unwilling to accept school district assertions concerning the appropriateness of a student's program absent proof in the form of data (Zelin, 2000). A review of recent decisions concerning progress monitoring reveals five primary areas of concern regarding progress monitoring:

PROGRESS MONITORING IS ESSENTIAL TO EVALUATING THE APPROPRIATENESS OF A CHILD'S PROGRAM, YET THERE IS LESS COMPLIANCE WITH THIS REQUIRED COMPONENT OF THE IEP THAN ANY OTHER.

- The IEP team fails to develop or implement progress monitoring plans;
- Responsibilities for progress monitoring are improperly delegated;
- The IEP team does not plan or implement progress monitoring for behavior intervention plans (BIPs);
- The team uses inappropriate measures to determine student progress towards graduation; or
- Progress monitoring is not frequent enough to meet the requirements of IDEA or to provide meaningful data to IEP teams.

Lack of Plans for Progress Monitoring

IDEA 1997 clearly required that a student's IEP include a plan for progress monitoring, yet many IEPs have been deemed inadequate—to the extent of denying students with disabilities an appropriate education—because of a lack of such plans or a failure to implement them.

In *Pennsbury School District* (2000), the hearing officer concluded that an IEP lacked "adequate statements regarding how [the student's] progress toward the annual goals will be measured" (102 LRP 10466) and that the IEP was not reasonably calculated to provide educational benefit to the student. The hearing officer in *Escambia County Public School System* (2004) issued a stronger decision, concluding:

> The most glaring deficiency was the absence of a notation as to whether [the student] had mastered any of his benchmarks . . . without the dates of mastery of benchmarks indicated on the IEP a parent cannot determine the progress that the child has been making during the school year . . . it is crucial that a parent (or other IEP member) be able to examine the IEP document to see if satisfactory progress is being made toward the attainment of the student's annual goals and if not, whether there is a need for adjustments to his program (42 IDELR 248).

Another state administrative review officer noted that "simple checkmarks indi-cating progress rather than regression or achievement of [the student's] goals" did not meet the requirements of IDEA, and ordered the IEP team to reconvene and draft an IEP with "objective measures of measuring progress" (*Rio Rancho Public Schools*, 2003, 40 IDELR 140).

IDEA 1997 CLEARLY REQUIRED THAT A STUDENT'S IEP INCLUDE A PLAN FOR PROGRESS MONITORING, YET MANY IEPS HAVE BEEN DEEMED INADEQUATE TO THE EXTENT OF DENYING STUDENTS WITH DISABILITIES AN APPROPRIATE EDUCATION BECAUSE OF A LACK OF SUCH PLANS OR A FAILURE TO IMPLEMENT THEM.

Responsibility for Progress Monitoring

Progress monitoring is the responsibility of the IEP team. At the time an IEP is developed, it must specify and document plans for progress monitoring, including what will be monitored, who will monitor, when and where the monitoring will be conducted, and how the data will be reported.

Although paraprofessionals and aides may assist in data collection for progress monitoring, the IEP team is charged with determining if the child's progress is sufficient. Two administrative decisions from Iowa highlighted the duties of IEP teams concerning progress monitoring. In *Sioux City Community School District v. Western Hills Area Education Agency 12* (2003), the administrative law judge concluded that the school district failed in its responsibility to monitor progress of a seven-year-old child with autism who was fully included in a general education first-grade classroom. Although the paraprofessional was involved in data collection, the special education teacher specified on the IEP to monitor progress did not regularly observe in the general education classroom and did not monitor or record progress toward goals. The administrative law judge determined that the "confusion of roles and responsibilities of IEP implementation and progress monitoring" may have been an "artifact of insufficient planning" for the child's full inclusion (103 LRP 37969). Similarly, in *Linn-Mar Community School District v. Grant Wood Area Education Agency 10* (2004), a 19-year-old student with autism was placed with an associate who was responsible for instruction, behavior management, and data collection. Yet the IEP team failed to document his progress, although the parents provided extensive documentation of the student's behavior deterioration and the inadequacy of his special education program. The administrative law judge (ALJ) concluded that

> The progress monitoring data presented by the school district is vague for certain IEP components and nonexistent for others. Few meaningful data are available to help the IEP team review progress or confidentially convince this ALJ that the programs offered to [the student] were calculated to provide meaningful benefit (41 IDELR 24).

The parents were awarded 3 years of compensatory education.

AT THE TIME AN IEP IS DEVELOPED, IT MUST SPECIFY AND DOCUMENT PLANS FOR PROGRESS MONITORING, INCLUDING WHAT WILL BE MONITORED, WHO WILL MONITOR, WHEN AND WHERE THE MONITORING WILL BE CONDUCTED, AND HOW THE DATA WILL BE REPORTED.

Behavior Intervention Plans

Both IDEA 1997 and the IDEIA of 2004 require IEP teams to consider factors including "in the case of a child whose behavior impedes his or her learning or that of others, consider, when appropriate, strategies, including positive behavioral interventions, strategies, and supports to address that behavior" (20 U.S.C. § 1414(d)(3)(B)(i)). The intent of the provision is to develop proactive, preventive approaches to behavior problems rather than reactive or punitive responses such as time-out or suspension (Bartlett, Weisenstein, & Etscheidt, 2002).

Although neither IDEA nor federal regulations specified the components of a behavioral intervention plan (BIP), the administrative law judge in *Mason City Community School District v. Northern Trails Area Education Agency 2* (2001) concluded that a BIP must be based on assessment data, be individualized to meet the child's unique needs, include positive behavioral support strategies, be implemented as planned, and be monitored to determine the effect of the planned interventions. Another administrative law judge determined that the lack of specificity and progress monitoring for a BIP for a young child with Asperger's syndrome rendered the IEP inappropriate (*West Des Moines Community School District v. Heartland Area Education Agency*, 2002). The IEP team must "assess what is or is not working for [the student] whom everyone has agreed is dealing with significant behavioral challenges" (36 IDERL 222).

Progress Toward Graduation

Case law has clarified that in order to graduate a student with a disability under IDEA, the student must meet a district's general graduation policies and achieve sufficient progress toward IEP goals and objectives (*Kevin T. v. Elmhurst Community School District No. 205*, 2001).

In *Black River Falls School District* (2004), a hearing officer concluded that although the student met general graduation requirements, he failed to make progress on IEP goals and objectives. No objective criteria were used to determine progress, and the district failed to make a determination about the sufficiency of progress and the student's readiness to graduate.

Frequency of Reporting Progress

IDEA requires that the IEP must include a statement of how the child's parents will be regularly informed of both progress toward goals and the extent to which that progress is sufficient (20 U.S.C. § 1414(d)(1)(A)(viii)). Teams must also report progress "at least as often as parents are informed of their nondisabled child's progress" (20 U.S.C. § 1414(d)(1)(A)(viii)(II)).

Two decisions found that the frequency of progress monitoring was inconsistent with IDEA's requirements, or was not frequent enough to provide the IEP team with meaningful data. In *Alta Loma Elementary School* (2002), a school district failed to report a student's progress toward IEP goals three times during the year, the frequency that parents of nondisabled children were informed. Although this did not result in denial of an appropriate program, the student's parents argued that without such information, they were not able to participate fully in the development of their child's IEP. The 19-year-old student with a progressive muscular disorder in *Del Norte County Unified School District* (2000) required frequent data collection and quarterly assessments of his communication skills. The hearing officer concluded that frequent assessment of communication progress would provide the IEP team "with the accurate assessment data needed to make any changes necessary in [the stu-

dent's] communication devices and/or communication goals and objectives" (33 IDELR 50).

Improving Progress Monitoring for Students With Disabilities

Develop Plans for Progress Monitoring That Include Multiple Measures

The IEP team must select an appropriate progress monitoring approach for each student goal or objective. Simple checkmarks or arrows as progress indicators are insufficient. If checkmark summaries are used, they must be based on data collected and accessible to the IEP team, and should include direct measures, indirect measures, and authentic measures of progress.

Direct measures may include behavior observation or curriculum-based assessment (CBA). Behavior observation is a valid index of student performance and assists in progress monitoring; techniques include frequency recording, duration recording, interval recording, and time sampling (Maag, 2004). CBA is an evaluation of a student's performance in the specific curriculum employed by the school. The method involves direct observation of performance and repeated recordings of student response (Hargrove, Church, Yssel, & Koch, 2002). Criterion-referenced tests (CRT) and curriculum-based measurement (CBM) are two types of CBA measures. CRTs are teacher-constructed tests to assess student performance in a hierarchy of skills from the curriculum (Jones, 2001). A CBM is a set of standard, simple, short-duration fluency measures of reading, spelling, written expression, and mathematics to assess key indicators of student achievement (Shinn & Shinn, 2001). Direct measures provide valid and reliable indications of student progress.

Student progress may also be monitored with *indirect measures* to supplement the direct, objective methods. Indirect measures include rubrics, goal attainment scaling, or student self-monitoring. Rubrics are useful measures of student performance for a variety of goals and objectives. A rubric describes performance competencies on a Likert-type scale with both qualitative and quantitative descriptions. For example, a rubric for a writing goal may include a performance description ranging from "fresh and vigorous" to "nonspecific and immature" in evaluating word choice or from "clear descriptions and explanations" to "completely lacking" in evaluating story development (Schirmer & Bailey, 2000, p. 54). Variations of rubric-based measures include T-charts (Stanford & Reeves, 2005), spelling rubrics (Loeffler, 2005), and mnemonic rubrics (Jackson & Larkin, 2002). Goal attainment scaling (GAS) is similar to a rubric approach; it involves rating student responses on a 5-point scale of best-to-worst outcomes. For example, the scale for a student goal of accuracy may include a range from totally correct to totally incorrect, and the scale for a goal concerning compliance to teacher directions may range from never to always. GAS provides a "time efficient and user-friendly" account of student progress (Roach & Elliott, 2005, p. 15). Teachers may use GAS daily as a repeated measure of student progress, or students might use the scale as a self-monitoring measure.

Student self-monitoring is another index of progress. Students can be cued to monitor behavior and to record the occurrence or nonoccurrence of the behavior. Self-monitoring has been used extensively in school settings (Wheeler & Richey, 2005), but is rarely considered as a source of progress monitoring data for IEPs.

Progress monitoring may also be enhanced by including *authentic measures of performance*. Informal conferences with students help teachers assess student performance (Alexandrin, 2003). Teachers may summarize the conversations in anecdotal notes included in a student's IEP file. Portfolio approaches to progress monitoring might also be considered; student work samples may provide important indicators of progress toward IEP goals. Students should be involved in the construction and evaluation of their portfolio work (Kleinert, Green, Hurte, Clayton, & Oetinger, 2002). Assistive technology can be used to help construct portfolios for students with severe

disabilities (Denham & Lahm, 2001). Similarly, videotaping can effectively supplement other measures, and may be shared with parents to show a child's level of performance and improve parental awareness of the child's progress (Hundt, 2002).

Specify the Who, Where and When of Progress Monitoring

After identifying the IEP goals and settling on progress measures, the IEP team must specify how the progress monitoring plan will be implemented. This includes identifying the individuals responsible for data collection, along with the location, dates, and time of data collection. Although paraprofessionals and aides may assist in data collection, the IEP team is responsible for decisions concerning the adequacy of student progress. Certain members of the IEP team may be responsible for direct measures such as behavior observation (e.g., a school psychologist), and teachers, parents, or students may collect indirect measures. Members of the IEP team who are responsible for implementing IEP goals should also be responsible for monitoring progress toward those goals. The team should also establish frequency of data collection, to provide sufficient data for evaluating the student's progress.

> THE IEP TEAM MUST SPECIFY HOW THE PROGRESS MONITORING PLAN WILL BE IMPLEMENTED, IDENTIFYING THE INDIVIDUALS RESPONSIBLE FOR DATA COLLECTION, ALONG WITH THE LOCATION, DATES, AND TIME OF DATA COLLECTION.

Monitor Both Academic and Behavioral Goals

Often academic goals for students with disabilities are specified in the IEP document, and behavioral goals are included in a BIP. Plans for evaluating BIP effectiveness should include both direct and indirect measures (Wheeler &

Improving Progress Monitoring

- Develop plans for progress monitoring that include multiple measures.
- Specify the who, where, and when of progress monitoring.
- Monitor both academic and behavioral goals.

Richey, 2005). As with academic goals, the BIP should clearly specify the "who, where, and when" for progress monitoring.

> MEMBERS OF THE IEP TEAM WHO ARE RESPONSIBLE FOR IMPLEMENTING IEP GOALS SHOULD ALSO BE RESPONSIBLE FOR MONITORING PROGRESS TOWARD THOSE GOALS.

IEP teams must also recognize graduation as an academic goal, and plan to collect data supporting a student's readiness for graduation. Importantly, IDEIA requires that appropriate, measurable postsecondary goals be developed for students with disabilities (20 U.S.C. § 1414(d)(1)(A)(i)(VIII)). Progress monitoring of postsecondary goals helps to ensure that transition plans and services are appropriate and that students with disabilities are "prepared to lead productive and independent adult lives" (20 U.S.C. § 1404(c)(5)(A)(ii)).

Final Thoughts

The 2004 reauthorization of IDEA ensured that progress monitoring remain a required component of an IEP; other provisions mandated greater accountability for student progress. The President's Commission on Excellence in Special Education highlighted the importance of adequate progress monitoring in several findings. One recommendation was to increase a focus on results: "IDEA will only fulfill its intended purpose if it raises its expectations for students and becomes results-oriented . . . judged by the opportunities it provides and the outcomes achieved by each child" (President's Commission on Excellence in Special Education, 2002, p. 8).

Progress monitoring is a vital component of an IEP and essential to evaluating the appropriateness of a child's program. By improving progress monitoring, IEP teams will ensure that the educational programs developed for students with disabilities will be meaningful and beneficial.

References

Alexandrin, J. R. (2003). Using continuous, constructive classroom evaluations. *TEACHING Exceptional Children, 36*(1), 52–57.

Alta Loma Elementary School, 102 LRP 31876 (SEA CA 2002).

Bartlett, L. D., Weisenstein, G. R., & Etscheidt, S. (2002). *Successful inclusion for educational leaders.* Upper Saddle River, NJ: Prentice-Hall.

Black River Falls School District, 40 IDELR 163 (SEA WI 2004).

Code of Federal Regulations (1999). Assistance to States for the Education of Children with Disabilities and the Early Intervention Program for Infants and Toddlers with Disabilities; Final Regulations. Washington, DC: U. S. Department of Education.

Del Norte County Unified School District, 33 IDELR 50 (SEA CA 2000).

Denham, A., & Lahm, E. A. (2001). Using technology to construct alternate portfolios for students with moderate to severe disabilities. *TEACHING Exceptional Children, 33*(5), 10–17.

Escambia County Public School System, 42 IDELR 248 (SEA AL 2004).

Hargrove, L. J., Church, K. L., Yssel, N., & Koch, K. (2002). Curriculum-based assessment: Reading and state academic standards. *Preventing School Failure, 46*(4), 48–51.

Hundt, T. A. (2002).Videotaping young children in the classroom: Parents as partners. *TEACHING Exceptional Children, 34*(3), 38–43.

Individuals With Disabilities Education Act, 20 U.S.C. § 1400 to 1491 (1997).

Individuals With Disabilities Education Improvement Act, 20 U.S.C. § 1400 to 1482 (2004).

Jackson, C. W., & Larkin, M. J. (2002). RUBRIC: Teaching students to use grading rubrics. *TEACHING Exceptional Children, 35*(1), 40–45.

Jones, C. J. (2001). Teacher-friendly curriculum-based assessment in spelling. *TEACHING Exceptional Children, 34*(2), 32–38.

Kevin T. v. Elmhurst Community School District No. 205, 36 IDELR 202 (ND IL 2001).

Kleinert, H., Green, P., Hurte, M., Clayton, J. & Oetinger, C. (2002). Creating and using meaningful alternate assessments. *TEACHING Exceptional Children, 34*(4), 40–47.

Linn-Mar Community School District v. Grant Wood Area Education Agency 10, 41 IDELR 24 (SEA IA 2004).

Loeffler, K. A. (2005). No more Friday spelling tests? An alternative spelling assessment for students with learning disabilities. *TEACHING Exceptional Children, 37*(4), 24–27.

Maag, J. W. (2004). *Behavior management: From theoretical implications to practical applications* (2nd ed.). Belmont, CA: Wadsworth.

Mason City Community School District v. Northern Trails Area Education Agency 2, 36 IDELR 50 (SEA IA 2001).

Peck, A., & Scarpati, S. (2005). Instruction and assessment. *TEACHING Exceptional Children, 37*(4), 7.

Pemberton, J. B. (2003). Communicating academic progress as an integral part of assessment. *TEACHING Exceptional Children, 35*(4), 16-20.

Pennsbury School District, 102 LRP 10466 (SEA PA 2000).

President's Commission on Excellence in Special Education (2002). *A new era: Revitalizing special education for children and their families.* Washington, DC: U.S. Department of Education.

Rio Rancho Public Schools, 40 IDELR 140 (SEA NM 2003).

Roach, A. T., & Elliott, S. N. (2005). Goal attainment scaling: An efficient and effective approach to monitoring student progress. *TEACHING Exceptional Children, 37*(4), 8–17.

Schirmer, B. R., & Bailey, J. (2000). Writing assessment rubric: An instructional approach for struggling writers. *TEACHING Exceptional Children, 33*(1), 52–58.

Shinn, M. M., & Shinn, M. R. (2001). Curriculum-based measurement: Cheaper, faster, and better assessment of students with learning disabilities. In L. Denti and P. Tefft-Cousin (Eds.), *New ways of looking at learning disabilities: Connections to classroom practice.* Denver, CO: Love.

Sioux City Community School District v. Western Hills Area Education Agency 12, 103 LRP 37969 (SEA IA 2003).

Stanford, P., & Reeves, S. (2005). Assessment that drives instruction. *TEACHING Exceptional Children, 37*(4), 18–22.

West Des Moines Community School District and Heartland Area Education Agency, 36 IDELR 222 (SEA IA 2002).

Wheeler, J. J., & Richey, D. D. (2005). *Behavior management: Principles and practices of positive behavior supports.* Upper Saddle River, NJ: Merrill Prentice-Hall.

Yell, M. (1998). *The law and special education.* Upper Saddle River, NJ: Prentice-Hall.

Zelin, G. M. (2000). *Educational benefit and meaningful progress under the new IDEA.* Paper presented at the Fourth Annual Iowa Special Education Law Conference, Des Moines, IA.

Susan K. Etscheidt *(CEC IA Federation), Associate Professor, Department of Special Education, University of Northern Iowa, Cedar Falls.*

Address correspondence to Susan K. Etscheidt, University of Northern Iowa, 655 Schindler Education Center, Cedar Falls, IA 50614 (e-mail: susan.etscheidt@uni.edu).

TEACHING Exceptional Children, *Vol. 38, No. 3, pp. 56–60*

- What is progress monitoring? How will progress monitoring affect how we work?

- How will it effect teaching and learning?

- Why is progress monitoring essential in the special education process?

The Seven Steps to Progress Monitoring the IEP

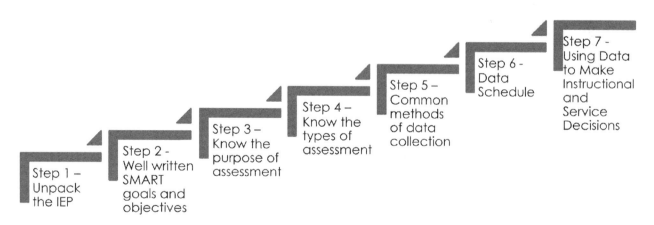

These seven components are necessary to create sound decisions based on meaningful data. We will be reviewing each in detail.

Step 1: Data Collection Unpack the Existing IEP

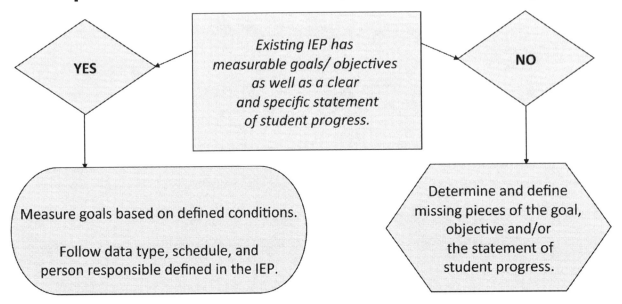

Step 1 – How do you know if your IEP is measurable, clear and has specific statements?

Activity

Directions: Think of a single goal or short term objective. Describe what data would be collected, how data would be collected, and how mastery would be determined. Below is a list of sample goals for your review.

Unpacking IEP Goals – Sample IEP Goals

Goal 1: Tyler will independently use at least three different organizational strategies (task initiation, planning, goal-directed persistence) to pass four academic classes as measured by quarterly report cards.

Goal 2: Tory will identify emotional stressors and coping strategies independently to decrease emotional irregularity from two to one times per month by June 2014 as measured by student self- assessment.

Goal 3: Jay will interpret the meaning of words encountered in text to respond to inferential questions after reading grade level text with at least 70% accuracy as measured by teacher created measures.

Goal 4: Aiden will sequence compound and compound/complex sentences to produce clear and coherent written responses in performance tasks to earn a rubric score of six out of eight.

Goal 5: Val will indicate basic needs, choices and wants in three different settings with familiar and unfamiliar individuals and give one additional verbal prompt by June 2014 as measured by a teacher created checklist.

Goal 6: Dan will remain on task for at least 20 minutes during both teacher directed and independent assignments or activities with no less than two verbal prompts in three out of four trials as measured by data collection charts.

Goal 7: Bryson will apply grade level phonics and word analysis skills to increase his guided reading level from an H to an L as measured by a benchmark assessment.

Goal 8: Angela will fluently use addition and subtraction to solve problems within 20 with 80% accuracy as measured by fact fluency probes.

Goal 9: Luis will answer comprehension questions related to grade level content to increase proficiency from 68% to 80% as measured by data collection charts.

Goal 10: Kim will decode regularly spelled CVC and VCE words in isolation and in context to increase from 60% to 80% accuracy as measured by teacher made tests.

Step 2: Make sure you have set S.M.A.R.T. goals and objectives

Strategic and Specific

Measurable

Attainable (within reach in time frame)

Results Oriented (focused on student learning)

Time Bound (by when?)

Reflection

- Strategic and Specific – What does each of those words mean?

- How will you know if you are strategic and specific?

- Measurable – What are examples of good measurable goals?

- Attainable – This means that goals and objectives can be mastered in a reasonable amount of time. A goal is not attainable if a student has the same goal year after year. Have the participants review a student's file. How did the goals change over a three year period?

- Results oriented – Define/describe the results to be determined.

- Time bound – What are the time factor parameters?

SMART Goals and Objectives

Ideally, a well-written goal should include the specific behavior or skill that the student will demonstrate, indicate the expected level of mastery and the measurement. It is also important to include a reference to the student's present level of performance and state if the expectation for this goal and increase or a decrease in performance of the skill if appropriate.

Activity

Directions: Identify each "SMART" component in the goal and objectives below. Using colored markers or highlighters, underline and label each "SMART" component.

- **Goal:** Jay will create one accurate prediction after reading grade level passages in two academic areas three out of five times as measured by a teacher created rubric.

- **Objective:** Given a prediction routine during note taking, Jay will record answers to questions in a complete sentence to earn a score of at least ¾ on a teacher created rubric in five consecutive attempts.

- **Objective:** Given a sentence starter, Jay will orally state a prediction to a peer or teacher to earn a rubric score of at least ¾ in four consecutive attempts.

CCS RL 2:1

Purpose of Assessment

"Great educators use assessment data to make real time decisions and to restructure their teaching accordingly."
- DOUGLAS B. REEVES

Reflection

- What does the Reeves quote mean to the special educator or to the IEP implementer?

- Is the special educator the only IEP implementer in all cases?

- Who else can or should be an implementer?

- How is that accomplished?

- What information or collaboration is needed for more than one implementer?

Step 3: Know the Purpose of Assessment

"No single assessment can meet everyone's information needs... To maximize student success, assessment must be seen as an <u>instructional tool</u> for use while learning is occurring, and as an <u>accountability tool</u> to determine if learning has occurred... Because both purposes are important, they must be in balance."

- NEA: BALANCED ASSESSMENT: KEY TO ACCOUNTABILIY AND IMPROVED STUDENT LEARNING, 2003

Assessment vs. Evaluation

- Assessment - the collection of data through the use of multiple measures.

- Evaluation - the process of integrating, interpreting, and summarizing the comprehensive assessment data, including indirect and preexisting sources.

NJCLD 2010

In Order to Collect Data

- Your IEP must have true data alignment.

- You must have SMART goals and objectives.

- Your PLAAFP must have useful information (for a refresher on the PLAAF, go to Module 1).

The PLAAFP and IEP Goals

- The PLAAFP contains your **baseline** data

- The goal/objective contains your **target** data

- The evaluation criteria describes **how** you will **collect** the **data**

- The data collection schedule outlines when you have to make decisions based on collected, analyzed and tabulated data

- What's missing? Collection, analyzing and tabulation…

Reflection

- What is a data collection schedule?

- How often should you collect data for an IEP?

The Blueprint: Building Powerful IEPs to Increase Student Achievement

Consider this – If you are "updating" the data in an IEP on a quarterly basis, how often would you need to collect data to gather data for four out of five trials? A good graph needs to include a minimum of five data points.

Activity: Analyze and Decide

1. Do your IEPs meet the data collection criteria?

2. What do you need to make your goals and objectives measurable?

3. How do you currently collect, chart and analyze data?

4. Could a teacher who does not know your student determine what kind of data you would collect based on how your IEP is currently written?

5. Could that teacher know how often? If not, how can we make the IEP more specific/measurable?

Activity: "List and Rank"

Directions: Below LIST all the important assessments you administer to students during the year. RANK each assessment as a 1, 2, or 3 in terms of having an <u>actual impact on instruction and student learning</u>. *"1" having the greatest impact and "3" having the least impact.*

Do not complete the Assessment column yet

Diagnostic – Assess understanding before instruction, planning

Formative – Provide guidance and feedback for students and teachers

Summative – Communicating about performance

Assessment	Rank 1-3 1= greatest impact 3= least impact	Comments	Type of Assessment D=Diagnostic F=Formative S=Summative

Reflection

- Are general grades the same as specific IEP skills data?

- Do standardized assessments give professionals the same information as formative assessments?

Step 4: Know the Type of Assessment You Will Use

- Diagnostic

- Formative

- Summative

Any of the three types can be designed as a performance assessment.

Reflection

- Can you list some diagnostic, formative and summative data for reading comprehension, fluency, vocabulary, executive function skills, problem solving, behavior or mathematics?

Diagnostic Assessment

- Used to *assess student level of understanding before instruction or when intervention is needed*

- May be traditional or performance based

- In some cases standardized tests may be used or modified

- Most important purpose is instructional *planning*

Formative Assessment

- Planned checks to see how student learning is progressing

- *Measures "a few things" frequently*

- May be traditional or performance based

- Most important purpose is *to provide feedback and guidance for students and teachers*

Summative Assessment

- A formal assessment at the conclusion of instruction

- *Measures "many things" infrequently*

- May be traditional or performance based

- Most important purpose is *communicating about performance*

Activity: Diagnostic, Summative and Formative Assessment

Directions: Return to the chart where you listed and ranked your assessments. Identify the type of assessment and indicate the type in the last column on the right.

Reflection

- What assessment area do you need to grow?

- What category of assessments do you feel has the greatest impact on instruction and student learning?

Criteria for Identifying Essential Common Outcomes
This answers "what should students learn?"

- Endurance

- Leverage

- Readiness for Next Level of Learning

- Douglas Reeves

Endurance – beyond a single test date – proficiency in reading, math and writing. *Are students expected to use the skills/knowledge long after the test is completed?*

Leverage – proficiency in creating graphs, tables, charts, being able to write an analytical essay. *Is this skill/knowledge applicable to many academic disciplines?*

Readiness – print awareness and sound symbol correspondence for beginning readers, reading comprehension and math fact recall for third grade to fourth grade. *Is this skill/knowledge preparing the student for success in the next grade/course?*

Reflection

- Why are these "ingredients" important to assessment and data collection?

Step 5: Three Common Methods for Data Collection

- Direct Measurement

- Indirect Measurement

- Authentic Measurement

Step 5: Data Collection—Direct Measurement

Direct Measurement provides valid and reliable indications of student progress.

Behavior Observation

Curriculum Based Assessment (CBA) is the direct observation and recording of student's performance in the school curriculum.

What are the two types of direct measures?

1.

2.

Ways to Record Student Behavior:

- Frequency recording

- Duration recording

- Interval recording

- Time sampling

- ABC

Step 5: Data Collection—Indirect Measurement

Indirect Measurement can supplement direct measures.

1. Rubrics

2. Goal Attainment Scaling

3. Interviews

4. Student Self-Monitoring

Step 5: Data Collection—Authentic Measurement

Authentic Measurement provides evidence os student performance through genuine student input.

1. Work Samples

2. Portfolios

3. Student Interviews

    • How can this be quantified?

Activity: Do You Have?

Directions: List your Direct, Indirect and Authentic Measurement Tools

If you need additional measurement tools, what are they and how can you get them?

Step 6: Data Collection Schedule

Indirect Instruction or Support

- Times for data collection should be worked into the time when service is being delivered, if possible.

- Data can also be collected remotely by other educational team members or service providers.

Consultation

- General education teachers and other service providers play a key role in data collection and input.

- Times for data collection should also be scheduled.

Step 6: Data Collection Schedule

- The effectiveness of services and instructional method is determined most efficiently when progress is measured frequently.

If progress is monitored	Then effectiveness may
Daily, as part of instruction	Be determined within 2 weeks
Twice a week	Be determined within a month
Weekly	Be determined within a quarter
Quarterly	NOT be determined, even after a year

If you want to be efficient and effective in your instruction, you will need to collect data more often.

Reflection

- How do general education teachers collect data under Response To Intervention?

- Should special education data collection be more intense, minimal or at the same level?

Step 6: Data Compilation Schedule

- Depends upon the data collection frequency

- Suggested compilation schedules:

If data is collected	Then data should be compiled
Daily	Weekly
Two or Three times per week	Bi-weekly or monthly
Once a week	Monthly

Now that you understand the need to collect data more frequently, it is important for you to understand that you need to compile that data and analyze the trend to determine if instruction is working. For example, a teacher was regularly collecting data about a student's ability to organize his materials for the day and collect the correct daily period schedule to follow. When the teacher finally compiled and analyzed the data, she found that the student had mastered the goal some time ago and was ready for a more demanding expectation.

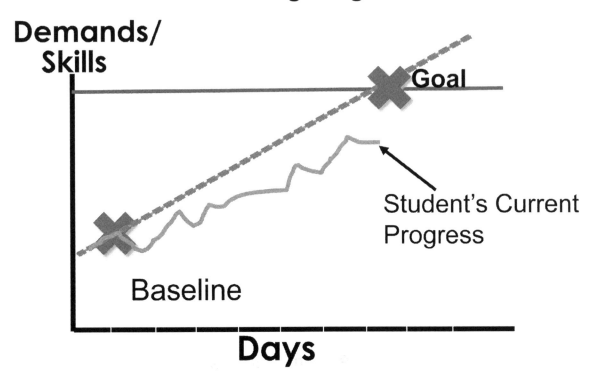

Monitoring Progress

Graphing data will provide a quick picture of how well the student is doing relative to the potential line of growth. In this example the student is making progress, but it is slower than expected.

Reflection

- Do you think the student will eventually reach the goal?

- How much more time do they think is needed?

- Is this intervention working?

The Blueprint: Building Powerful IEPs to Increase Student Achievement
All Rights Reserved/ www.crec.org

Instructional Decisions Based on Data

- **6-8 data points of progress monitoring** are required to make an informed decision about student progress or lack thereof. (McCook, 2006)(Brown-Chidsey & Steege, 2005)

Reflection

- How do we collect data in order to progress monitor?

- Look at an IEP. How often do you need to schedule data collection?

- Can you use items/processes already in place?

General Decision-Making Framework

4-Point Rule (McCook 2006) is a tool to help determine if the student is on track to meet the target that you set for proficiency for meeting the goal or objective. As you collect data, you can determine the trend toward the likelihood of the student mastering the goal/objective at this level by analyzing the last four data points. For example, if your benchmark is for the student to complete a particular task with 80% accuracy by the end of the term of the IEP, then that would be your goal line. As you collect data about the student's progress toward this goal, you can see a trend through the last four data points that will indicate if the student is likely to achieve that goal in the time that you have set aside.

If a minimum of three weeks of instruction have occurred and at least six points have been collected, then examine the four most recent data points. If all four points are:

- above goal-line, then increase goal.

- below goal-line, then check fidelity and make an adjustment in intervention.

- both above and below the goal-line, then keep collecting data until trend-line rule or 4-point rule can be applied.

Step 7: Four Aspects of Using Data to Make Decisions

1. Progress

   - Did the student make the progress expected by the IEP team? (criteria)

2. Comparison to Peers or Standards

3. Levels of Independance

4. Goal Status

   - Will work in the goal be continued?

   - Will student be dismissed from the goal area?

Activity

- What is your current data collection schedule?

- Are there any technologies you can use to help you with data?

Activity

Use one of the tools below or other tools that you are familiar with to create a graph.

- www.chartdog.com

- Kid's Zone – Create A Graph

- Excel or word tables

- iPad apps

- Google Forms

Resources for Finding the Most Up-To-Date Data Collection Tools

1. www.educatorstechnology.com - Med Kharbach – Med manages this website, a Facebook page, Pinterest page and Twitter account. He posts tips, guides, tutorials, reviews and lists of great tools for teachers need to be successful with classroom technology.

2. www.k12mobilelearning.com – This website also has a Facebook page. Posts update visitors on recent releases and useful tools for teachers.

3. www.freetech4teachers.com – Richard Byrne writes an award winning educational sharing blog. He also has a Facebook page.

4. ITunes App Store – The App Store has an Education category that is also broken down by several subcategories. Data collection tools can be found in Education, Special Education and Apps for Teachers.

5. www.appsineducation.blogspot.com – Greg Swanson posts apps that can be found in each key learning area in the App Store. He also posts on Twitter.

6. http://www.appolicious.com/curated-apps/1111-special-education-data-collection-tools - This website curates a list of apps that can be used by special education teachers to collect data.

Activity: Data Analysis

Directions: Select a student goal or objective that you are assessing. Go back to the chart that you created using the sample data or your own data. Use this chart as a way to answer these questions. The KU-CRL Data Collection Worksheet can be used to help organize this process.

Student Goal or Objective:

- How will the data inform/drive instruction?

- What is the student's performance?

- What progress did the student make?

- Is the rate of progress satisfactory for continuous growth? For closing the achievement gap?

- When will the data be revisited?

- What additional data do you need?

- Do you have enough data to answer these questions confidently?

The Blueprint: Building Powerful IEPs to Increase Student Achievement

- Do they have data that they can share with families to support their instructional decisions?

The KU-CRL Data Collection Worksheet

Data Collection Plan

School: _____ Student: _____

Date:_____ Case Manager:_____

STEPS of Data Collection	Action Steps	Person(s) Responsible	Target Date
Step 1: Identify a Focus • Identify an area you are concerned about • Become more familiar with this topic • Focus on a specific issue causing problems • Specify the research based interventions you will use	Identify area of concern		
	Gather information (teacher reports, high stakes test data, assessment data)		
	Review and summarize information		
	Identify target issue (Academic, Behavioral, Social, Vocational, Language, Pragmatic, Physical…)		
	List potential interventions and intervention schedule (options)		

STEPS of Data Collection	Action Steps	Person(s) Responsible	Target Date
Step 2: Write Action Plan • Lay out what actions and measurements to take and what data to gather and when (mandated per IEP) • Determine who will do what tasks (tasks tied to classroom practices and tasks connected to interpreting the data) • Lay out what actions and measurements to take and what data to gather and when • Determine who will do what tasks (tasks tied to classroom practices and tasks connected to interpreting the data)	What: Specify classroom practices that will be implemented (Direct instruction, embedded through co-teaching…)		
	How: Identify data to be collected (Gen ed, Classroom, Self-contained, Other support…such as ESL, School Psy., SLP…)		
	Identify parameters that will be used to collect data (i.e. 10 minutes in Eng class, or small group in resource)		
	Identify who will be recording data		
	Set data collection timeline		
	Identify how data will be collected and shared (i.e. para will collect once a week and give to case manager every Friday)		
Step 3: Collect Data • Determine data collection points (calendar) • Identify data collection tools (tally, rubric, portfolio…) • Identify multiple types of data for stronger findings: student artifacts, preassessments, reflective journals, student interviews, peer observations, information from student records	Identify data types for collection		
	Identify schedule for data collection		
	Identify data analyses time line		

The Blueprint: Building Powerful IEPs to Increase Student Achievement

STEPS of Data Collection	Action Steps	Person(s) Responsible	Target Date
Step 4: Organize the Data (an ongoing process) • Organize data for quality research findings (efficiently, practically, and protective of sensitive or confidential information) • Create graphs, charts and other visual representations of the data	Create visual representation of data		
	Clearly identify labeling information		
	Enter data		
Step 5: Analyze and Interpret Data; Draw Conclusions (an ongoing process) • Consult with colleagues like specialists, guidance counselors, gen. ed teachers, administrators... • Consider both qualitative and quantitative data • Examine what happened before and after the intervention/ specialized instruction	Identify and consult with colleagues		
	Identify patterns and themes related to trend lines, aim lines and benchmarks		
	Identify success points against target dates		
	Summarize findings		
	Other:		
	Conclusions		
Step 6: Share Findings (Optional) • Share with identified stakeholders • Collaborate with colleagues/staff to gain fresh perspective on conclusions drawn	Share with stakeholders Yes or No		
	Share with person with fresh perspective Yes or No		
	Other		

STEPS of Data Collection	Action Steps	Person(s) Responsible	Target Date
Step 7: Develop a New Action Plan • How can practices change? • Determine if additional strategies/interventions are needed • Consult IEP and update • If mastery is apparent, suggest new goals based on data or IEP adjustment. • If mastery is not apparent, hypothesize why and revise/edit plan.	Is the intervention working?		
	Is there a need to continue change or alter plan drop the strategy or intervention Explain		
	What practices should be changed as a result of this information? What additional strategies/interventions should be tried? Hypothesis for new strategies or interventions:		

Adapted for data use by Sonya Kunkel, SIM Professional Developer-Capitol Region Education Council, CT, January 2010. PGraner.MTipton – KUCRL 2009 International SIM Conference. Lawrence, Kansas. July 15-17, 2009. Adapted from: Brighton, C. M., & Moon, T. R. (2007). Action research step-by-step: A tool for educators to change their worlds. *Gifted Child Today, 30*(2), 23-27. Also see: Brighton, C.M. (2009). Embarking on action research. *Educational Leadership. 66(5),* 40-44.

Step 7: Analyzing Data

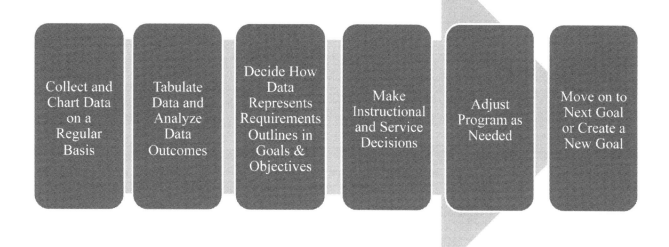

| Collect and Chart Data on a Regular Basis | Tabulate Data and Analyze Data Outcomes | Decide How Data Represents Requirements Outlines in Goals & Objectives | Make Instructional and Service Decisions | Adjust Program as Needed | Move on to Next Goal or Create a New Goal |

How Data Drives Your Teaching

Requires you to:

- Focus lesson plans

- Adjust transdisciplinary matrices

- Plan collaborative and data collection times

- Chart/graph data

- Share data

- Change how you work?

Improved data collection will allow teachers and related service personnel to develop an accurate PLAAFP that is more likely to predict the rate of learning for a student with a disability. This leads to IEP goals and objectives that are more likely to result in educational benefit. This data can be collected and used in a variety of service settings

(i.e. self-contained, resource, supported general education classrooms, non-supported general education classrooms, co-teaching classrooms)

What is your current data plan?

Refocus on IEP goals and objectives.

- How is your data reflected in your paperwork?

- How do you plan for your data in your lesson plans?

Experts often possess more data than judgment.
-COLIN POWELL

Reflections to Inform Your Practice

1. Summarize the important aspects of Collecting Data and Monitoring the IEP Progress.

2. What practices am I going to apply in my job or what experiences will I try?

3. What did I try and did it work. Why or why not?

4. What will I try next?

Assess Your Learning

Module 4 – Collecting Data and Monitoring of the IEP Progress

1. Should general educators be expected to collect data toward progress on IEP goals and objectives?

2. Does the IEP team need to reconvene if the student is not making progress on the goals and objectives or masters goals and objectives before the annual review date?

Answers to Assess Your Learning

Module 4 – Collecting Data and Monitoring of the IEP Progress

1. **Should general educators be expected to collect data toward progress on IEP goals and objectives?**

   Yes. Many teachers are concerned about increasing the work load of a colleague by expecting them to collect data on IEP goals and objectives. However, the general education teacher is a part of the team and does provide direct instruction to the student with an IEP. It is important for teams to consider what data is already available that will document the progress toward goals and objectives. This may alleviate the concern about an additional form or procedure that is above and beyond the progress monitoring data that may already be collected during the course of that instructional block.

2. **Does the IEP team need to reconvene if the student is not making progress on the goals and objectives or masters goals and objectives before the annual review date?**

   Yes. Changes to the child's program should be addressed in an IEP planning meeting. There may be some circumstances in certain states in which an addendum to the IEP can be created without a formal meeting. It is important to review the state and federal regulations that dictate the conditions for reconvening the IEP team meeting.

Online Resources, Bibliography, and Glossary

ONLINE RESOURCES

- Educational Benefit Case Law –
  http://www.harborhouselaw.com/articles/rowley.reexamine.johnson.htm
  http://www.wrightslaw.com/law/caselaw/case_Evans_Rhinebeck_FAPE.html

- Creating Useful Individualized Education Programs
  www.ldonline.org/article/6276/?theme=print

- Writing the PLAAFP
  http://www.aaps.k12.mi.us/siss.procedures/files/step_by_step_guide_to_writing_plaafp_statements.pdf
  http://www.gvsu.edu/autismcenter/iep-development-and-implementation-for-students-with-asd-94.htm

- State Department of Education on Counseling
  http://www.sde.ct.gov/sde/lib/sde/PDF/DEPS/Special/counseling.pdf

- Writing Social, Emotional and Behavioral Goals
  http://www.asdk12.org/depts/SEL/Media/SEL_standards.pdf
  http://www.state.nj.us/education/ccss/progressions/2-2-A.htm

- Hunt Institute Video Viewing Guide
  http://www.hunt-institute.org/elements/media/files/CCSS_Video_User_Guide_FINAL_for_upload.pdf

- Resource Guide to the Massachusetts Curriculum Frameworks for Students with Disabilities www.doe.mass.edu/mcas/alt/resources.html

- Common Core Essential Elements for English Language Arts
  dpi.wi.gov/files/sped/pdf/assmt-ccee-english-wodescr.pdf

- Dynamic Learning Maps Essential Elements for Mathematics
  www.school.utah.gov/sars/docs/sscd/ee_math-draft.aspx

BIBLIOGRAPHY

An Administrator's Guide to Measuring Achievement for Students with IEPs. http://www.
awa11.k12.ia.us/iep/iepresults/AdministratorsGuide.htm

"A Seven Step Process to Creating Standards Based IEPs." *IDEAS That Work*. Project
Forum NASDSE, n.d. Web. 7 Dec. 2012. <www.nasdse.org/Portals/0/SevenStepProc
esstoCreatingStandards-basedIEPs.pdf>.

Ainsworth, Larry. *"Unwrapping" the standards: a simple process to make standards
manageable*. Denver, CO: Advanced Learning Press :, 2003. Print.

Blanton, L. , Pugach, C., Florian, L. (2011), Preparing general education teachers to
improve outcomes for students with disabilities. (policy number not given). AACTE
Policy Brief, May 9, 2011

Brown-Chidsey, Rachel, and Mark W. Steege. Response to Intervention: Principles and
Strategies for Effective Practice. New York: Guilford, 2005. Print.

Conzemius, Ann, and Jan O'Neil. "The Power of SMART Goals: Using Goals to Improve
Student Learning." *Solution Tree*. N.p., n.d. Web. 30 Jan. 2012. <www.solution-tree.
com/media/pdf/study_guides/SMART_Goals__Study_Guide.pdf>.

Crawford, Linda. "Accommodations vs. Modifications: What's the
Difference?"Accommodations vs. Modifications. National Center for Learning
Disabilities, n.d. Web. 29 July 2013.

Davis Holbrook, Marla. "Standards-Based Individualized Education Program." *InForum*.
National Association of State Directors of Special Education, 1 Aug. 2007. Web. 10
Dec. 2012. <projectforum.org/docs/standards-basediepexamples.pdf>.

"General Directions to Use the State's Model Individual Education Program (IEP)." *P-12:
NYSED*. N.p., n.d. Web. 9 Jan. 2012. <http://www.p12.nysed.gov/specialed/formsno-
tices/IEP/directions.htm>.

Hall, T., Strangman, N. & Meyer, A. Differentiated Instruction and Implications for UDL Implementation, National Center for Accessible Instructional Materials, Jan. 2011

"IEP Process Guide." *Massachusetts Department of Education*. N.p., n.d. Web. 9 Jan. 2012. <www.doe.mass.edu/sped/iep/proguide.pdf>.

Jackson, R. (2010). What are the needs of students with low-incidence disabilities. Curriculum Access for Students with Low-Incidence Disabilities: The Promise of Universal Design for Learning (p. 15). Washington, D.C.: National Center on Accessing the General Curriculum.

Jones, M.M. (2001, October). An Introduction To Data Collection, SWO SERRC, Cincinnati, OH.

Kortering, L. J., McClannon, T. W., & Braziel, P. M. (November/December 2008). Universal design for learning. A look at what algebra and biology students with and without high incidence conditions are saying. Remedial and Special Education, 29(6), 352-363.

MacQuarrie, Patricia. "Standards-Based Individualized Education Programs (IEPs) Benefit Students Â« FOCUS on Results." FOCUS on Results. N.p., n.d. Web. 7 Dec. 2012. <http://focus.cenmi.org/2009/06/01/ standards-based-individualized-education-programs-ieps-benefit-students/>.

McCook, J.E. (2006). *The RTI guide: Developing and implementing a model in your schools*. Horsham, PA: LRP Publications

National Education Association. (2003). Balanced Assessment: The Key to Accountability and Improved Student Learning (Student Assessment Series). Retrieved July 29, 2013 from http://www.assessmentinst.com/forms/nea-balancedas-sess.pdf

Nelson, Chelie, and David Lindeman. "Curriculum and the IEP." *Kansas University*. N.p., n.d. Web. 30 Jan. 2012. <www.kskits.org/ta/Packets/RoleOfCurriculum/6_Curriculum AndTheIEP/6_1CurriculumIEP.pdf>.

Nolet, V., & McLaughlin, M. J. (2000). Accessing the general curriculum: including students with disabilities in standards-based reform. Thousand Oaks, Calif.: Corwin Press.

"Parent's Guide to Special Education in Connecticut." *Connecticut State Department of Education*. N.p., n.d. Web. 9 Jan. 2012. <www.sde.ct.gov/sde/lib/sde/PDF/DEPS/Special/Parents_Guide_SE.pdf>.

Powers, E. (2013) "How Will the Common Core Change What We Do?" Edutopia, 2/5/13 retrieved from the internet

"Procedure Manual Teacher Edition." *Section 7 Educational Benefit*. N.p., n.d. Web. 30 Jan. 2012. <www.sjcoe.org/selpa/files%5Cteachermanual7.pdf>.

"Professional Standards." *Council for Exceptional Children*. N.p., n.d. Web. 16 Jan. 2012. <www.cec.sped.org/Content/NavigationMenu/Professional Development/ProfessionalStandards/>.

"Programs & Services : Special Education : Special Education Forms." *Vermont Department of Education*. N.p., n.d. Web. 9 Dec. 2012. <http://education.vermont.gov/new/html/pgm_sped/forms.html#iep>.

"Programs & Services: Special Education Forms Instructions." *Vermont Department of Education*. N.p., n.d. Web. 18 Jan. 2012. <education.vermont.gov/documents/EDU-Special_Ed_Forms_Instructions.pdf>.

Sandall, S., Giacomini, J., Smith, B.J., & Hemmeter, M.L., (Eds.). (2006). DEC recommended practices toolkits [CD-ROM]. Missoula, MT: Division for Early Childhood of the Council for Exceptional Children. Retrieved from internet 6/10/13

Smith, S. "Creating Useful Individualized Education Programs (IEPs)." *LD OnLine: The world's leading website on learning disabilities and ADHD*. N.p., n.d. Web. 2 Feb. 2012. <http://www.ldonline.org/article/6276/?theme=print>.

Swearingen, Richard. "A Primer: Diagnostic, Summative, & Formative Assessment." 2002. TS. Heritage University. June 2010. Web. 29 July 2013.

United States. National Joint Committee on Learning Disabilities. Comprehensive Assessment and Evaluation of Students With Learning Disabilities. N.p.: n.p., n.d. Print.

United States. Council of Chief State School Officers. Oklahoma Accommodations Manual for Instruction and Assessment How to Select, Administer, and Evaluate the Use of Accommodations for Instruction and Assessment of Students with Disabilities. By Sandra J. Thompson. [Oklahoma City]: Oklahoma State Dept. of Education, Special Education Services, 2010. Print.

Wright, Peter W. D., Pamela Darr Wright, and Sandra Webb Connor. *All about IEPs: answers to frequently asked questions about IEPs*. Hartfield, Va.: Harbor House Law Press, 2010. Print.

GLOSSARY

Accommodation: Accommodations should not change expectations of the curriculum for a specific grade level. Accommodations are services and/or teaching supports that students may need to demonstrate learning. Accommodations are designed to provide equity, not advantages for students. Some examples of accommodations include: extra time for assignments or tests, the use of taped textbooks, and study carrel.

Benchmark: Benchmark in education is essentially learning targets that are set up that identify what a student should know. Often benchmarks are used to indicate the specific steps or targets to reach a particular learning outcome.

Formative Assessments: Formative assessments are ongoing assessments, reviews, observations used in a classroom. Formative assessments are used to improve instructional methods and student feedback throughout the learning process. The results of formative assessments are used to validate instruction as well as give key information for modifying instruction to meet learner needs.

Functional Performance: Functional performance is often related to routine activities of everyday living. Some examples of functional performance are: behavioral, social emotional, physical, and daily living skills.

Goals: (2)(i) A statement of measurable annual goals, including academic and functional goals designed to – (A) Meet the child's needs that result from the child's disability to enable the child to be involved in and make progress in the general education curriculum; and (B) Meet each of the child's other educational needs that result from the child's disability... [§300.320(a)(2)(i)(A) and (B)] Also defined as, written statement in a student's individual education plan (IEP) that is chronologically age appropriate, specific to a curricular or functional need and is achievable, measurable and meaningful for the student's current and future environments.

Modification: Modifications are changes made to curriculum expectations in order to meet the needs of the student. Modifications are made when the grade level or age appropriate expectations are beyond the student's level of ability. Modifications may be minimal or very complex depending on the student's performance. Modifications must be clearly acknowledged in the IEP (CT State Special Education Parent Guide, 2007).

Objectives: Objectives are no longer required for all students. Objectives are required for students with significant cognitive delay and who have been identified in need of being alternatively assessed. Objectives are short term benchmarks that are in alignment with meeting a specific goal. Measurable intermediate steps between present level of performance and the stated goal; basis for developing a detailed plan.

Summative Assessment: Summative assessments are typically used to evaluate the effectiveness of an instructional program and/or services. The goal is to make a judgment of student competency after instruction has been completed. Summative assessments inform what the student has mastered and identify any further instructional needs.

Universal Design for Learning (UDL): Process of designing instruction that is accessible by all students; UDL includes multiple means of representation, multiple means of expression, and multiple means of engagement; the focus in creation of UDL curricula is on technology and materials.

Educational Resources

BUILDING POWERFUL SPECIAL EDUCATION PRACTICES

The Blueprint offers over sixteen training modules on relevant special education topics related to:

- Common Core Standards
- Individual Education Plans
- Transition
- English Learners with Disabilities
- Instruction
- Inclusion and Collaboration

Building Powerful IEPs to Increase Student Achievement Workbook

This comprehensive workbook is for the aspiring or practicing special education and related services staff. Packed with easy-to-implement strategies and ideas for building IEPs

EDUCATORS' TOOLBOX

Resources for Improving Student Outcomes

Evaluators' Guide to Conducting Educational Program Reviews

This comprehensive workbook gives the rationale, standards, and step-by-step instructions on how and when to use various evaluation tools. It includes evaluation methods and practices with case studies, as well as the tools you will need to perform your own specialized program evaluation or to work with other evaluators.

Assistive Technology Guide to Maximizing Learning for Students with Autism

A valuable resource for all aspiring or practicing special education or regular education teachers, paraeducators, therapists, and families. It contains information on twelve relevant topics like overview and consideration of assistive technology, and assistive technology for communication.

Response to Intervention:
Planning and Implementing a Multi-Tiered System of Support

This Book provides a school-wide apporach, with real-world examples and practical solutions, to implementing Response to Intervention. This guide is an effective tool and road map to assist school educators in developing RTI models for their school or district.

THE COMPASS

Helping Paraeducators Navigate the Profession

A comprehensive job-embedded professional development curriculum designed for paraeducators

Basic Modules:

- *Roles and Resposibilies*
- *Ethics and Legal Issues*
- *Instructional Strategies*
- *Communications*
- *Managing Behaviors*

The COMPASS Basic Modules workbook is packed with easy-to-implement strategies and ideas for aspiring or practicing paraeducators, and is aligned with the National Paraeducator Standards. It gives the paraeducator tools and sample forms to have that "first" conversation with their teacher at the beginning of the year and helps maintain communication. The basic workbook covers all five Basic Modules listed above.

Advanced Modules include:
Curriculum and Instruction

- Advanced Instructional Strategies
- Connecting Instruction to the Common Core Standards
- Creating Independent Learners
- Scientific Research Based Intervention (SRBI) and the Role of the Paraeducator
- Supporting Literacy Instruction
- Supporting Math Instruction

School and Community Climate

- Advanced Behavioral Strategies
- School Climate: Creating Environments that are Safe for All
- Health and Wellness for the Effective Paraeducator

Other Modules

- Assitive Technology to Support Student Learning
- Effective Paraeducator Supervision
- Exceptional Learners
- Job Coaching
- Teaching English Language Learners
- Teaching Students with Autism

For detailed information, please contact
Margaret MacDonald Ph.D.,
Director of Technical Assistance and Brokering Services,
mmacdonald@crec.org
or 860-524-4037,
or Tricia Silva, Program Manager,
tsilva@crec.org or 860-524-4085

For more information or to purchase any of these educational resources, please scan the QR code below, or visit www.crec.org/tabs/order

Made in the USA
San Bernardino, CA
11 June 2016